Jan Morris was born in 1926, of a Welsh father and an English mother. She spent the last years of her life with her partner, Elizabeth Morris, in the top left-hand corner of Wales, between the mountains and the sea. Her books include *Coronation Everest*, *Venice*, the Pax Britannica trilogy and *Conundrum*. She was also the author of six books about cities and countries, two autobiographical books, several volumes of collected travel essays and the unclassifiable *Trieste and the Meaning of Nowhere*. In 2018 she was recognised for her outstanding contribution to travel writing by the Edward Stanford Travel Writing Awards, and published *In My Mind's Eye: A Thought Diary*.

Praise for *Thinking Again*:

'*Thinking Again* [is] composed of daily diary entries that unlock Morris's storehouse of memory as they describe children in coffee shops or dogs on the beach at Pwllheli . . . The tone is of someone who has seen the whole world and decided on this place as an ending.' *Observer*

'There's a warmth to the writing, a companionship made possible between the author and the reader which makes the book itself a sort of kindness, a two-hundred-page gift.' *Nation Cymru*

'Morris's love for Wales provides perhaps the surest, most personal comfort, in f--- -f - universal difficulty, an awareness that days bot'-

under Venetian skies o

'Regardless of the subject matter, Morris has a knack for provoking introspection . . . This extraordinary woman finds traces of kindness everywhere . . . She also practices it in her own life, continually demonstrating a fresh, altruistic sensibility that we could all learn from.' *Wales Art Review*

'There are flashes of vivacity . . . an acerbic wit and gentle playfulness . . . [Morris] is surely to be applauded for her indomitable spirit.' *Irish Times*

---

by the same author

HEAVEN'S COMMAND: AN IMPERIAL PROGRESS
PAX BRITANNICA: THE CLIMAX OF AN EMPIRE
FAREWELL THE TRUMPETS: AN IMPERIAL RETREAT
COAST TO COAST
CORONATION EVEREST
VENICE
OXFORD
CONUNDRUM
TRIESTE AND THE MEANING OF NOWHERE
A WRITER'S HOUSE IN WALES
A WRITER'S WORLD
EUROPE: AN INTIMATE JOURNEY
HAV
FISHER'S FACE
DESTINATIONS
A VENETIAN BESTIARY
SPAIN
AMONG THE CITIES
THE GREAT PORT
THE HASHEMITE KINGS
HONG KONG
LINCOLN
THE MATTER OF WALES
MANHATTAN '45
THE MARKET OF SELEUKIA
SOUTH AFRICAN WINTER
THE SPECTACLE OF EMPIRE
CONTACT!
CIAO, CARPACCIO!
BATTLESHIP YAMATO
IN MY MIND'S EYE

JAN MORRIS

THINKING AGAIN

faber

First published in 2020
by Faber & Faber Limited
Bloomsbury House, 74–77 Great Russell Street
London WC1B 3DA

This paperback edition published in 2021

Designed by Faber
Printed and bound by CPI Group (UK) Ltd, Croydon, CR0 4YY

All rights reserved
© Jan Morris, 2020

The right of Jan Morris to be identified as author of this work
has been asserted in accordance with Section 77 of the Copyright,
Designs and Patents Act 1988

This book is sold subject to the condition that it shall not, by way of trade or
otherwise, be lent, resold, hired out or otherwise circulated without the pub-
lisher's prior consent in any form of binding or cover other than that in which
it is published and without a similar condition including this condition being
imposed on the subsequent purchaser

A CIP record for this book
is available from the British Library

ISBN 978–0–571–35766–6

FSC
www.fsc.org
MIX
Paper from
responsible sources
FSC® C020471

2 4 6 8 10 9 7 5 3 1

With Kind Regards to Everyone

DAY 1

Ave et Vale?

My indulgent publishers, in both London and New York, published the first 188 of these diary entries in book form. Since entry 188 ended cheerfully but distinctly elegiacally, it occurred to me that perhaps that was the moment to stop writing my diary altogether.

However I am a strong believer in the strength of Routine, and conceiving and writing these inconsequential little pieces has become virtually mechanical in itself, like many another petty compulsion. My mother, who was partly of Quaker stock, would never dream of placing another volume on top of her Bible, and pagan agnostic that I am, I still find myself involuntarily touching wood (i.e. touching the wood of the Cross) to avert bad luck. And I don't know about you, but in my everyday affairs too there are personal routines, edging into such superstitions, that I feel I must honour.

For example nothing would induce me to go to bed without calling a last Goodnight to my Elizabeth, and at this moment I really have to re-read another chapter of dear old *Anna Karenina* before I turn the lights out. Rain or shine, sleet or snow, I have to perform my daily walk (and the worse the weather, the more strict the compulsion), while indulging in Wednesday's allotted marmalade at Tuesday's breakfast really would be more blasphemous than merely irreverent.

And this daily diary has edged its way into the roster. It has become a pleasant part of my life – not a duty, nor even a chore, but a happy few minutes each day whenever I feel like it. Whether or not it goes well (and I know when it doesn't), I offer it to my readers, as to myself, with doubts and apologies often, but always with a smug conviction of Routine honoured.

So there it is. Not *Vale* just yet!

For most people around the world, it seems to me, these weeks around the beginning of spring 2018 have been one long, disorienting cock-up, and it has knocked many of our disciplines askew . . . Tragedy to farce, incompetence to despotism, uncertainty to arrogance, all that is most miserable about the human condition seems to have entangled all our lives as the winter ends. The weather hasn't helped either, what with typhoons and forest fires and unprecedented snowfalls all over the place – schools closed, electric power failed, trains and flights cancelled, melting snow turned maliciously into floods. Nature itself seems to have had enough of us, and has told us so.

Worst of all, though, has been the way humanity has turned upon itself. Across the globe in these unhappy weeks there have been reports of corruptions and cruelties, killings, betrayals, reputations ruined and sneaky disclosures gleefully trumpeted. Is nobody decent any more? Can I not trust my neighbour? Where's God gone, if there is one? We don't know, we don't know, and there's the trouble. We have no certainties any more, no heroes to trust, no Way (in mystic capital letters) and no Destination.

But perhaps you will forgive me, on this wretched day, if I propagate an old thesis of my own once more. It is this: that the simplest and easiest of virtues, Kindness, can offer all of us not only a Way through the imbroglio, but a Destination too.

DAY 3

It being a sunny, boisterous day, for a change, I went for my thousand morning paces along the nearby waterfront of Pwllheli, where a hundred yachts are moored now and where long ago fleets of merchant schooners came and went.

My tune for the day, part whistled, part sort of sung to myself, was a song called 'Over There', which George M. Cohan wrote in 1917 to support American intervention in the European war. It's a fine confident march with a fine confident lyric, composed in the days when an American soldier posted overseas might be sure of a welcome wherever he went. He knew that whatever cause he was sent to support would be a just cause, and it was only proper that, as Cohan hymned it, he should not come home till it was over over there:

> *Over there, over there . . .*
> *The Yanks are coming*
> *. . . And we won't come back till it's*
> *over over there!*

Cohan died in 1942, so he did not live to know the irony that attends the song now, but as I walk I sing it anyway, if only in my mind's ear, to remember the greater days of a nobler nation.

Necrophilia is not one of my failings, but I do like grave-yards and memorial stones and such. I long ago wrote our own gravestone epitaph, which reads as follows: 'HERE ARE TWO FRIENDS, JAN AND ELIZABETH MORRIS, AT THE END OF ONE LIFE'. The inscribed stone awaits the day under the stairs, and will eventually be laid upon an islet we own in the river Dwyfor below our house, smilingly to crack and crumble into nothing.

Lots of people, of course, of every religious persuasion, do not want your standard hearse, wreath, sermon and cemetery kind of end, and near us here there is a place dedicated to burials of a very much simpler kind. It is a patch of conifer woodland, off a quiet country road, which shows no apparent sign of being consecrated or, for that matter, of being a burial place at all. I went there for the first time the other day, because it sounded like rather my sort of necropolis, but, alas, found it more disturbing than comforting. The wood was certainly peaceful, as I wandered through its shades. There was nobody else about, and no sound but the breath of the wind through the trees. At first there seemed to be no sign of human exploitation either, but gradually I realized that here and there, half hidden among the tree trunks, were small rough-cut stones with names on them, and occasional small bunches of flowers. It was as though my eyes were just getting used to the dark and silent peacefulness – those few scores of stones, scattered silent all among the trees, with their occasional remembrances . . .

But they were occasional. Those flowers were few, those names were often far off the track and had a lonely feel. There was peace, that's for sure, but it was like a peace of neglect, or even forgetfulness. Nature was all around that patch of wood, but it felt to me like Nature uninterested, and I found myself, as I returned to the car and the road, pining unexpectedly for a homely old gravestone with a rhyme from a hymn on it, a loving, simple message and a fresh bunch of shop-bought tulips, wrapped in cellophane.

DAY 5

Well, you must take my word for it, I did record a Thought for today, but when I re-read it the entry turned out to be so footling that I have expunged it with a muttered curse.

DAY 6

Talking of words, have you used 'algorithm' lately? It has only recently entered my ken, and seems to be on the make. The moment it enters my reading matter, on the screen or on the page, I am wary: I fear that there is discomfort to come, either because the reading matter is going to be too intellectual for me, or because the use of the noun (assuming it is a noun) portends pretensions to come. It's a pity, because I like the word itself, with its graceful shape and obvious Arab origins, but alas it is not yet my style.

Not yet. In the meantime, I have been exploring it. It means, the *Shorter Oxford English Dictionary* on my desk tells me, a set of rules used in problem-solving operations; or, as *Webster's* puts it, the art of calculating with any species of notation.

Of course the big *Oxford* downstairs, in all the swank of its fourteen volumes, has more to say about the word: for a start, that it doesn't exist, having 'passed through many pseudo-etymological perversions' as a mere corruption of 'algorist'. There are heaps of varied interpretations and explanations on the Web, but I have reached the suspicion that often enough people who use the word don't really know much more than I do about its meaning.

Never mind. 'Algorithm' is a lovely word, a noble, graceful word, and it moves me to learn that it comes (I don't quite know how) from the ninth-century surname of

Abu Ja'far Mohammed Ben Musa. I can't find him in my *Encyclopedia of Islam*, but I think I'll start using the word myself, algoristically, just to amuse him.

DAY 7

Today's news concerned, as it so often does, President Trump of the USA. Since his election he has seldom been out of our thoughts, has he not? This morning it seems he has done something good, I forget exactly what. It may turn out to be bad anyway, and by the time you read this you will, of course, know the result better than I do, but I venture now to record once more my own feelings about this equivocal man. I have always rather liked his political style, as against his personal ideals, which are almost grotesquely crude. He states his political case, whatever it is, boldly and unpretentiously to his own particular audience, and to hell with everyone else. It is an All-American way: America First! Make America Great Again! As one with a sneaking sympathy for patriotism, whatever flag it flies, I respond to this approach as instinctively as any redneck bigot.

Then again, although I loathe Trump's attitude to women, I think there is something forgivably childlike to his behaviour, like the sulks and outbursts of a spoilt schoolboy. He must, I know, be a man of true abilities – how else could he have assembled his immense financial holdings? He's no fool, and in his political relationships he really does remind me of a precocious pupil cocking the snook at his elders and betters. Many a foolish adolescent grows up to be a responsible adult, and many a lesser villain repents his sins.

I can hardly think of Donald Trump as a great states-man. Can you? Surely not, but I can just imagine history remembering him as Trump the Redeemed.

Please God!

DAY 8

A breathless hush (to borrow a phrase I've always liked from dear old Henry Newbolt), a breathless hush hung over our lane this morning, when I set off on my statutory one thousand paces in the aftermath of the worst storm we've had for years.

The newspapers dubbed it the Beast from the East, because it reached us from somewhere like Siberia and until yesterday raged mercilessly all over our islands, causing miscellaneous havoc and unhappiness almost everywhere. Off I went on this bleak morning after to survey the effects of it, and what I mostly found was hush. I met nobody, I saw nobody. I felt all alone in the world, and the ground all around me was littered with toppled trees and broken branches, patches of broken glass and the occasional soggily abandoned agricultural carton. I felt like giving up, opting out, abandoning the land so wasted and forlorn, leaving it all to the birds and beasts and searching for some other way . . .

But no. There were a few bedraggled sheep munching in one of the Parrys' fields, and presently, as I walked on, birds began to call, first the usual anonymous kind of burbling, but then sporadic snatches of legitimate birdsong, and finally salvos from a brazen pair of woodpeckers, the machine-gunners of Nature – the first I have heard in 2018! They changed my mood in an instant. I quickened my step, turned at the end of the lane and started for home; and as I walked now I whistled my chosen marching tune of the day, which awoke the woodland around me and made even the bare branches rustle.

So it was not, as I rather expected, echoes from *The Waste Land* that saw me home to lunch, but a buoyant word of encouragement from old Henry Newbolt. 'Play up!' I heard his fastidious Victorian timbre reach me again, as I put my stick back in the rack. 'Play up! play up! and play the game!'

DAY 9

It has been a horrible day, as it happens, all cold drizzle and wind and sudden fierce rain squalls, but was I deterred from my daily habits? Certainly not. Just as duty calls me to write this diary, so after a lifetime of travel and challenge I arrogantly pride myself on my one thousand diurnal paces, come what weather may, and scorn those who stay whimpering indoors.

On the other hand, I am constantly astonished, and rebuked, by the variety of people I regularly meet out there as I swagger through squall and blizzard on our seafront. They are often just as old as I am, and all of them are at least as resilient. There are those, of course, who are prisoners of their dogs, obliged to give them their daily exercise, throw stones into the sea for them and play monotonous, footling games that confirm my preference for cats. And there are those like me who walk out there as a matter of personal compulsion, or perhaps in obeyance of doctors' orders.

Most of them, though, are there simply because they want to be, and those are the ones I admire. How admirable are the mums and dads who cheerfully cavort with their robust young families, while the water streams down the necks of their mackintoshes. How truly heroic the old lady who regularly turns up in her wheelchair, chuckling wryly in the rain! The children themselves, one and all, exult in the wet mess and flounder of everything, and make me feel that one day they will rule us well.

So my conceit is by no means tempered by the fact that a multitude, young and old, is at least as hardy as I am. On the contrary, I am proud to know myself a member of it, and to feel as Henry V did, when he sympathized with gentlemen comfortably in bed when they might have been out there with him, winning the Battle of Agincourt!

DAY 10

Glimpses of Literary Life

As an ageing *littérateur* I sometimes find it necessary to pursue payment for my work. This was the case recently in the matter of a really rather remarkable essay, concerning hyperbole in religious poesy of the English Middle Ages (or something like that). I had delivered it to its commissioning magazine several weeks before, had apparently not been paid for it, and thought it time to investigate the matter through my bank.

Well, I call it 'my bank' because it used to have a branch in our local town, until they abandoned that and obliged us all, even artistes of a certain age, to make a highly inconvenient bus or car journey to somewhere else altogether. A polite telephone operator regrets, anyway, that an unusual flow of customer business is delaying things this morning, and says how truly sorry she is for the consequent delay, which, as she rightly says, is inconveniencing so many of their tremendously valued clients. A profound silence now falls upon my inquiry. All I want to find out is whether I have been paid the modest fee I am expecting for that essay (especially imaginative, though I say it myself, in discussing the use of simile in the work of the Venerable Bede). Has the magazine used it or not? When at last a man at the bank comes on the line and asks if he can help me, I quote him the six-digit number I had extracted from an all-but-illegible scratch card they had sent me long ago, and my fifteen-digit customer number, and my Motivation Code in duplicate, and my sixteen-digit card number, and my nine-digit security number, and my preference code, and my account numbers. And then the whole lot all over again, because there was one letter too many in the second rendition of my Motivation Code.

There is a long silence. Then the operator returns. 'I'm putting you through to Remainder Accounts,' I think she says, in an understanding sort of way, for in the meantime she has discovered my date of birth, 'and it has been a pleasure assisting you, Jan' (for senior citizens should preferably be addressed by first names). Silence returns, interrupted only by intermittent blips and hiccups, until I decide to call it a day. 'Thank you for your kind help anyway,' I tell her, and she says it is always a pleasure to be of service to valued clients.

I still don't know if they have used my essay, but I do hope they will – it really is rather insightful. In any case, it's not the money I care about. Of course not. It is satisfaction enough to remember that alone I wrote that particularly sympathetic passage, near the end of page 8, about the influence of Cotswold folk music upon Early English canticles.

DAY 11

Fairly early in the morning these days aircraft often begin playing around in the skies above these parts, and their noise enlivens my wakening hours. It is not the steady drone of airliners on their way to Dublin or New York, nor the busy, useful clatter of helicopters, but decidedly more exciting morning calls, I always like to think, from young men up there practising their flying technique.

Only today did I discover more about them. Sitting in the waiting room of our local health clinic, waiting to have my ears syringed, from a selection of magazines mostly about symptoms and treatments I came across one with a colour photograph of a fighter aircraft on the cover. What a surprise! It turned out to be the house magazine, so to speak, of a military airfield not far from us, and from it I gathered more about the causes of those morning goings-on – advanced readiness, I now assumed, for our defence against bad people.

I am all for that, of course, but the happiest thing I discovered from that journal, before I was called to surgery, was this: that among the aircraft lately manoeuvring so exhilaratingly above my head had been a visiting squadron from Switzerland! Friendly Swiss fighters over Wales! Could anything be happier?

I thought of stealing the magazine from the clinic, just to show friends that I wasn't romancing or hallucinating, but no, I thought that would be letting the standards of the side down.

DAY 12

When long ago my youth was ending, and I came home from abroad with some cash in my pocket, I resolved for the first time in my life to buy a brand-new car.

We were briefly living in London then. I didn't know much about cars, and what I felt about the look of them was chiefly obtained during my walks of those days, which generally consisted of a stroll up and down Harley Street, the street of the doctors. Their consulting rooms were lined with the newest automobiles of the day, and as I surveyed them all in passing I determined that the ones I liked the best were some machines called BMWs, in those days nearly as new to England as they were to me. 'Ah well,' thought I, 'but think of the cost!' Soon afterwards I was taking a taxi in one of the English cathedral cities, I forget which, and I happened to mention to the driver that I was considering buying a new car. What would he get, I asked him, if he were me? 'Funny you should ask,' he said. 'I had the Bishop in the back of the cab the other day, and he told me he'd just bought a lovely car himself. It was a make that was new to him, and it was new to me too. It was something called a BMW.'

BMW! Susceptible as I was, and am, to celestial commands, I went away and eventually bought one for myself, and I agreed with the Bishop. A lovely car it was, and we drove it with great pleasure, at home and abroad, until we decided we needed something more familial, so to speak, and traded it in for Volkswagen buses, and then, as middle age approached, I abandoned them too for my first boy racer, a Honda Civic Type R, which has been my dear friend ever since.

Nowadays my daily exercise often takes me along the promenade of our neighbouring seaside town, which in season is lined always with cars of every make – nearly all, it seems to me, virtually brand new. This is a good period, I think, for external automobile design. Most of these machines look elegant and discreet, and not at all vulgar. They represent the last generation of internal combustion cars, perhaps, before electricity and robotism take over, and this morning as I walked along the prom I asked myself which I considered the most elegant, discreet yet tough of them all.

Guess what! Yes, you said it, a BMW – the Bishop's choice! But I had no regrets, all the same, as I drove the old Type R, with an adolescent blast of its exhaust, up the hill and home.

It's Easter Sunday today, and for once the churches and chapels are full of faithful Christians celebrating the resurrection of their Lord. I am a sympathetic agnostic, and I rejoice with them, but I cannot help noting that this particular Easter Day, 2018, falls also on All Fools' Day.

I love and respect most of the Christian story, so full of kindness and sweet detail, pity and courage, children and animals and happy examples, but I just cannot accept the tale of Christ's resurrection from the dead either as fact or as moral motivation. To my mind it weakens the grandeur of one of the noblest monuments of literature, whether fact or fable, and offers us no inspirational exemplar.

It is hardly more persuasive, I think, than the famous April Fools' Day hoax which very nearly persuaded us (me included) that spaghetti grew on trees, or the tale that the astronomer Patrick Moore spun in 1976 about the forthcoming alignment of two planets – it would so alter the gravitational pull, he suggested, that everyone would be momentarily lighter at 9.47 a.m. that day (one woman reported that she and eleven friends had tried it and had all been gently elevated from their chairs and wafted around the room).

But the story of the Resurrection is, of course, more than a mere deception. It is, in my ignorant judgement, an unworthy fictional appendix to a magnificent work of art and morality, and may God forgive me if I am wrong.

DAY 14

Most of the symptoms of extreme old age I take in my stride as being tiresomely normal, but there is one that is, perhaps, peculiar to my calling. It is an honest confusion in the memory between fact and fiction, and it has cropped up lately concerning two things that I believe happened to me during the years of the 1940s, when I spent much time pottering around the territories of the old Soviet Union.

In the first memory I was going somewhere out of Moscow by train in the company of an assigned travel guide, whom I assumed to be an agent of the KGB. It was night-time in winter, the passing landscape was deep in snow, and as we stood together in the corridor I noticed through the window a solitary muffled young woman hurrying wildly up a lane.

'Who d'you suppose she's running away from?' I remarked to my companion, who replied at once, 'Probably from the secret police.' I realized then that she was tricking me into the belief that she was ideologically sympathetic, when she was really all too ready to ensnare me in some bad intention towards the State.

Nothing more happened. We arrived at our destination, wherever it was, and parted amicably – but the little episode was engraved in my mind as illustrative of the place and the time, and obviously I wrote about it.

Or did I? I can find no evidence at all, in all my books and travel articles, in all my notes and jottings, that it ever happened at all. Nor can I find any corroboration for another little Russian episode of my life, which happened in old Leningrad forty or fifty years ago. I had made the acquaintance, in a café, I think, of a youngish Russian who had been a pilot in the Red Air Force, and who struck me as a fine and soldierly sort of fellow. He lived nearby, and invited me to his flat to have a drink. Well, I thought, everything's grist to my mill, so I happily accepted and we walked together to a middle-sized residential block, the sort of respectable place the bourgeoisie would have occupied before the Revolution.

It had gone down in the world since then, and as we went up the stairs I looked through a half-opened door into what was evidently his bedroom. I found that he hadn't even made his bed. That citizen of stately Leningrad, that officer and Russian gentleman, hadn't bothered to make his bed. The very phrase went into my mind as a kind of theme for Stalin's Russia, and I stored it in my mind, as writers do, and later used it in an essay.

Or did I? I can find no written evidence of the phrase or, indeed, the episode among all the thousands of words I wrote about travelling in that lost place and age. Like the woman on the Russian train, the officer in the noblest of Russian cities seems to have vanished, somewhere between fact and fiction, among the grey murky symbolisms of the Cold War.

DAY 15

A marvellous day today, so we dropped everything and drove into the mountains to have lunch at the Pen-y-Gwryd inn – the legendary PYG beloved of mountaineers around the world, which stands on the very flank of Snowdon and has been an intermittent haunt of mine for sixty years or more. Today is a holiday, so the roads were jam-packed with cars and buses, and every lane and track we passed was full of hikers, climbers, picnickers and burbling infants. I loved it all – it seemed to me a sort of anti-inferno, portrayed by some mighty laughing artist sharing and portraying an uproarious festival of humanity.

But for me, all the same, the best moment of our ride into the mountains must have been the conception of some very different artist. It occurred when we rounded a sudden bend and discovered in a shadowy glimpse a family of wild goats – six or seven of them, young and old, silent, quivering and dappled among the trees. Just for a moment I saw them as an altogether separate revelation, portrayed by some genius of profounder temperament, before we hastened by to PYG. (Where I didn't get the Guinness I was looking forward to – because of some bureaucratic cock-up, their alcohol licence had temporarily expired.)

O tempora, o mores!

Here's an odd and unimportant little fancy for you. It concerns introductions to books.

In 1866, William Dean Howells, later to be popularly known as the Dean of American Letters, wrote a big two-volume book about Venice. He was in his thirtieth year, and when twenty-odd years later he published a new edition of the work, unsurprisingly he found much of it outdated. He decided, though, not to revise it, and this is how he explained himself in his new introduction:

> The book is distinctly a youthful book, for good as well as for ill. I might mend it; but I am afraid I should mar it if I meddled with it. I know its faults as I know the sins of my youth, and I hope to be forgiven in what it seems to be too late to undo.

Nearly a century later, in 1960, I too wrote a big book about Venice, and like Howells, years later I found it impossible to bring it up to date for a new edition. This is how I excused myself, more gushingly than he did!

> I cannot pretend that I feel about Venice as I felt when I originally wrote this book, and so I find that I cannot really revise it . . . It is Venice seen through young eyes, responsive above all to the stimuli of youth . . . I hope

28

this record of old ecstasies will still find its responses among my readers, and especially among those who, coming to the Serenissima fresh, young and exuberant as I did, will recognize their own pleasures in these pages, and see a little of themselves in me.

To be honest, I have never read another word of Mr Howells, and so far as I know he has never read a word of mine (he died in 1920), but I have always felt oddly close to him because of those twin apologias, and from time to time I still dip with comradely pleasure into my copy of *Venetian Life*, fourth edition, Boston and New York, MDCCCXCII.

DAY 17

A sort of fable today, from the life and with a happy moral.

The clutch of my old car let me down a few days ago, stranding me without my telephone in a fairly busy road on the outskirts of Cricieth, our nearest town. I sat there at a loss, feeling sorry for myself and evidently showing it, for after a time the young couple in a neighbouring house, one of a row of villas, noticed me sitting there morose. On the suggestion of his wife (so I later learnt) the husband came out to offer his help, and in no time he had the Automobile Association on its way to tow my car to the nearest garage, and had me thankfully at home.

Well, it so happened that on the day of that charity a new book of mine was published, so I thought it would be proper if I presented a properly inscribed copy to my benefactors, to commemorate the occasion. Off I went with a copy, with my message already written in it, and lo! for the life of me I could not remember which house in the row was theirs. I unsuccessfully tried four, one after the other, and in each house the occupants greeted me with mystified but amused concern, tried their best to identify which of their neighbours I needed, and expressed their regret that they couldn't have been the ones to have rescued me that day. One after the other they laughed with me and sent me none the wiser on my way.

Until at last I reached my fifth house, and it was the one. The husband was away at work, but the wife greeted me with infinite enthusiasm, and I produced my book, and unwrapped it for her, and read aloud to her the inscription I had written in it, thanking them both for their great kindness to a total stranger and offering the book as a token of my gratitude and true admiration.

She listened to me in silence, but when I handed the book over to her, she burst into tears. And my moral to the little tale? Only this: that in every row of houses, almost anywhere, in any country, decent people are living, only waiting to laugh, cry and be kind.

I only hope it's true.

DAY 18

'What is truth?' asked jesting Pilate, and sweet Jesus, on this day, 12 April 2018, he might well ask. By the time you read this entry it will all be history anyway, but to me, today, the whole world seems uncertain about the truth. Some pundits say we are simply on the brink of that terrible old calamity, world war, in this case the democratic West versus the despotic East. Other authorities tell us the truth of the world's confusion is infinitely more complex, and is entrammelled in hundreds of separate disputes, major and minor, justified or contrived, disputes peculiar to themselves or unimaginably generic, all mixed up with economics and political intelligence and infinite varieties of loyalty.

What is truth? Pontius Pilate, it seems, did not ask the question very seriously, and I suspect many of us this morning feel rather as he did, and wish perhaps that the United Nations could deliver a reply as absolute as did the High Priests on that day of judgement long ago.

But no, today is no day for jesting. We have no Christ among us to exemplify the truth for us all, nor even a Pontius Pilate to represent our quandaries. We must make up our own minds, and if I am anyone to go by, this morning we are floundering over our breakfasts.

Apropos of yesterday's hazy thoughts, here's an adden-
dum. Queuing for lunch at a takeaway place, I happened
to notice that the woman next to me was clutching her
credit card, as I was myself, in readiness to pay for our
victuals. 'Well,' she said, 'you never know, do you, anything might happen – did you not read the news this morning'? I agreed, anything might happen, and sure enough at
that moment an employee approached us and said curtly
that the food counter was closed. She didn't say why.
'You see?' we both exclaimed. 'Anything can happen, and
nobody says why!'

But I had lately been re-reading the autobiography of
an ancient hero of mine, General Sir William Butler (1838–
1910), and I remembered then what he thought about the
misty manipulators of events in his time. It was, he wrote,
not wild idealists, devious diplomats or ever-ambitious
politicians, let alone soldiers in the field, who pulled the
wires or inexplicably closed, as it were, the food counters
of his day. No, says the dear old boy (and remember, he
was writing in the 1830s), in the end we always find it is
the distant financier behind the scenes, the man of many
millions, the controller of vast enterprises, turning some
nebulous proposition into a vital question of the hour,
'whipping the whole pack together and letting loose the
dogs of war'.

I would have quoted him to the woman in the queue,
but she had gone off in a huff, packing away the evidence.

DAY 20

Talk of war and rumours of wars reminds me of how many I have lived through, whether near or far, during my own nine decades on this restless planet. Oddly enough, the one that I have experienced most vividly of all was fought before I was born.

I hardly knew my father, who died when I was eight or nine years old and already away at boarding school. His health had been broken and his life ruined by poison gas in France during the First World War – the Great War, as we used to call it – and the most vivid memory I have of him finds him fitfully asleep in bed one afternoon when I was home from school on holiday. In his dreams the war was raging still, and when I crept awestruck into his bedroom he cried out warnings, tossed and turned, moaned and coughed uncontrollably and sometimes bitterly laughed, so alive in his nightmare that I heard the guns myself, ducked to the screaming whistle of the shells, smelt the cordite and the treacherous, murderous gas . . .

He died soon afterwards, when I was back at school, and I well remember the day when the headmaster gently broke the news to me. My father has never quite died for me, though. I hardly knew him, but when I think of him, I am with him still, at his side, on that day of war in Flanders.

The most unfashionable person you can be in Britain today, and the most defamed, is a racist, but nevertheless I must admit to some twinges of the condition when I walk up our lane to the top. In fact, nowadays I seldom walk any further because of what I suppose must be classed as racist prejudice. For seventy years I have lived within the bounds of an ancient Welsh estate, long ago known as a Township, and recorded in 1352 as being inhabited by Einion ap Gruffydd and Lleuci, the daughter of Ieuan. You can't get much more Welsh than that, and with brief intermissions the district has remained absolutely Welsh ever since – farmed by Welsh families and profoundly impregnated, one might say, with Cymreictod, the intangible state of being that is Welshness.

Well, a few years ago a cottage not far away fell vacant. Not being rich I failed to buy it, and so probably for the first time since the days of Einion ap Gruffydd it became inhabited by Sais, Saxons – not Welsh at all, but English people!

They were nice people, polite and unobtrusive, but they were English people, and they rebuilt and developed that cottage in an English way. Doubtless without thinking about it they made it a little corner of England, washed by an English river, breathing English air. I am half English myself, and a sucker for Rupert Brooke, but nowadays, whenever I walk that way, I feel alienated. The old, old magic of the place, the ancient inheritance of Einion and Lleuci, is abruptly switched off, and at the first glimpse of the new crazy paving in the cottage garden, and the holiday caravan parked beside its bank of the river, and the ornamental city street lamp, I turn on my heel and go home to Cymreictod . . .

Is that racism? It probably is, but I'm not going to apologize, even in the language of Heaven . . .

I don't know about you, but I'm not against bad language in general. It depends on the circumstances – it fondly amuses me, for instance, to hear of Churchill in bed telling an intrusive child to bugger off. There is one swear word, however, that I do find distasteful in any circumstances, and unfortunately for me it has lately unescapably pro-liferated, at least in Britain. I hate to use it myself, but there we are, obviously I've got to name it now, and here it is: FUCK, with its adjectival derivative FUCKING, when employed not to describe sexual intercourse, but as an indeterminate expletive.

It has a long pedigree. Dr Johnson, I note, did not list it in his dictionary at all in 1755, but the *Oxford Dictionary* gives plenty of space to its use since the Middle Ages as a profane sort of word, extra-onomatopoeic, both the look and the sound of it representing its meaning – ugly in appearance, ugly to hear and ugly in function, a crude substitute for some more graceful and apposite profanity. And most of all I dislike the word FUCK when it comes from the mouth of a woman – seldom, I suspect, spontane-ously from the heart but, as it were, out of the ideology of liberation, a crude and coarse expression of a noble cause.

But PS, apropos of the Churchillian word, I remember from long ago a dubious naval story, the text of which I have long forgotten, but whose punchline I still find funny: 'You could have buggered me through me oilskins.'

DAY 23

Some time ago, I recorded a radio programme for the BBC which was intended to express my own feelings about the USA. It was the time of the Pax Americana, of the Special Relationship between Britain and America, and I had written a lot around the subject, so the programme was partly affectionate memoir and partly appropriate music. People seemed to like it, so I was invited to do a sequel, this time concerning another preoccupation of mine: the late British Empire.

Choosing music to go with the American programme had been easy enough – anything from 'Shenandoah' to Thelonius Monk – but orchestrating an equivalent response to my feelings about the British Empire was another matter. I had called the programme itself 'An Equivocation', and I needed a selection that reflected a similar abstraction – for if I am proud of lots about the British Empire, of course I know there is much to be ashamed of too.

Well, I had Elgar's 'Land of Hope and Glory', of course, first in stately grandeur and then in Jingo degradation at the Last Night of the Proms, and I had some pompous coronation music (Walton's 'Orb and Sceptre') and some self-mockery (Gilbert and Sullivan), and the programme ended with that sad old hymn about Proud Empires Passing Away. But the music that provided a happy surprise of equivocation, halfway through, was the Kipling ballad 'On the Road to Mandalay', with its robust imperialist refrain: 'Come you back, you British Soldier, Come you back to Mandalay, / Where the dawn comes up like thunder out of China cross the bay . . .'

I love the old song anyway, and I was especially pleased with the rendering of it that I found for my programme, because it was elegantly performed by a citizen of a country that had once been part of the British Empire itself but had long since thrown off the colonial coils.

The former colony was the United States of America. And the singer ('Ship me somewhere east of Suez, where the best is like the worst')? The singer was Frank Sinatra.

DAY 24

It was a glorious morning today, but unreliable. The sun shone, the sea was cobalt blue, the birds sang and my old darling thought it was just the day for an old-school picnic lunch – you know, like the ones we used to have.

Aha, but I knew better than that. I recognized the extra tinge in the wind that spoke of sudden showers, and so I decided instead upon a twenty-first-century picnic.

This is what we did. We went down to the supermarket and bought ourselves two platters of sushi, clean, cold, glittering from the ice box and with chopsticks, to go. And around the corner at a place called Bargain Booze we acquired two plastic cups of steaming coffee out of a humming machine.

We then we drove to a green, grassy spot at the edge of the sea below the castle, looking out across that cobalt blue to the green hills beyond our bay, and there we parked the car, all alone, and sat in it lordly, as though we owned the place. We switched the engine off, we turned the radio on to Classic FM, and sure enough – didn't I say so? – just as we started on the sushi the first traitorous raindrops began to fall.

Oh, there's a lot to be said for modernity! I myself have never been an eager picnicker, but really, what could have been much better than our lunch there today – that marvellous view in front of us, familiar melodies on the radio, the snug, warm, comfortable seats of the old Honda, the gentle pitter-patter of rain on its roof, Bargain Booze cappuccino still steaming and delicate morsels of raw seafood, icy and pungent, straight (well, more or less straight) from far Japan?

Wasn't it better than the crumbly sandwiches, lukewarm tea and biscuits that we might have been having in the old days? I certainly thought so, but I fear my beloved was still pining for the picnics we used to know and didn't even finish her pickled eel and tofu. The rain blobbed all over the car as I drove home, but bless her dear heart, I knew better than to say I told her so.

Today I offer you, by permission, an introduction to a language, Desperanto, which my collaborating son Twm has introduced me to. This is a page from an instruction book, *Desperanto Made Easy*, entitled 'Lesson 7, In the Café', and to get the hang of it you must imagine the specimen Desperantian dialogue being spoken by an instructor whose native language is a rather curious, semi-accented, slightly Australian sort of English. Here we go:

L.O.
L.O.2.U.2.
I.C.U.R.B.C.!
S.
F.U.N.E.M.?
A.?
I.Z.: F.U.N.E.M.?
O! S.I.F.M.N.I.F.X.
I.8.X.! F.U.N.E.T.?
S., I.F.T.
L.F.M.N.T.
OK.

Key to Lesson 7 tomorrow! Can you wait?

DAY 26

By now you probably have a better command of Desperanto that I have myself, but just in case, here's a plain English translation of yesterday's dialogue – in a café, you may remember:

HULLO.
HULLO TO YOU TOO.
I SEE YOU ARE BUSY!
YES.
HAVE YOU ANY HAM?
EH?
I SAID: HAVE YOU ANY HAM?
O! YES, I HAVE HAM AND I HAVE EGGS.
I HATE EGGS! HAVE YOU ANY TEA?
YES, I HAVE TEA.
I'LL HAVE HAM AND TEA.
OK.

It doesn't sound like much of a café, does it, but then I suppose Lesson 7 is only for relative beginners.

Another Glimpse of Literary Life

The arrival of a letter concerning royalties is always a pregnant moment for authors. Will it be encouraging or dismaying, urging them to yet higher accomplishment or making them murmur in despair over their computers, 'Dear God, what's the use of trying?' This morning I received such a challenge, concerning a modest book I wrote years ago about my house in Wales, and this, in brief, is what it told me. The little work, I was gratified to learn, had lately been published not only in the United States as well as in England, but also in translated editions in German, Japanese, Dutch, Spanish and Taiwanese. All had been gratifyingly recorded in the left-hand column of the statement, and my eyes slid expectantly to the right-hand column, where the financial proceeds were analysed. The list took into account, of course, exchange rates, agents' fees, publishers' advances, direct marketing and Electronic Books Escalation, and concluded with the following stately assessment of total profits from my book: £000.00.

DAY 28

Forty-three per cent of Quakers, I learn from one of the more esoteric of recent statistics, 'are unable to profess a belief in God'. Bravo, say I, because you can be quite sure that they are decent, intelligent people, and not atheist nutters.

I speak with feeling, because there are Quaker strains in my own hybrid origins, and I have always admired the element of restrained mysticism in their religious attitudes. I occasionally look in on their meetings, and shall never forget one in particular. It was in Oxford, on 23 November 1963. On the previous day President Kennedy had been assassinated, and that morning I looked in at the Quaker Meeting House in St Giles' Street. It was packed with Friends, sitting silent and thoughtful there, and only one solitary person rose to speak.

He was the head of one of the Oxford colleges, an eminent former diplomat, and he offered a prayer on behalf of the assassin.

DAY 29

A hideous day's news greets me this morning, of wars and rumours of wars, of sleazy capitalism and dubious diplomacy, democracy coarsened, loyalties abandoned, religions squabbling, footling gossip and squalid accusations. 'What's the use?' I say to myself, aloud and in the general direction of nowhere. I give up. Count me out. If I had a newspaper, I would scrumple it up and throw it in the fire, if I had a fire. As it is, I switch off the damned computer, curse a curse and compose this thought for the day.

Outside my window a soft wind is stirring the trees – themselves gently mutating into the green of a new summer.

Rather a creepy contribution today. I went to bed late, after a light supper and only a small glass of local cider, and switched my light off at midnight exactly, doing without my usual fascinating chapter of *Anna Karenina*. Instantly I went to sleep, and after a night's perfect, dreamless slumber, woke up this morning to the absolute conviction that it was my birthday, 2 October.

It was nothing of the sort, being in fact 13 May, but I was perfectly sure of it, and very nearly rang my neighbour at the farm, who shares a birthday with me, to swap mutual congratulations. Luckily I didn't, realizing just in time that I was in hallucination, but instead it strangely dawned upon me that although it was certainly not my own date of birth, it really was the birthdays of my two musician brothers, who both entered the world, though two years apart, on 13 May.

They both died long ago, and I can only suppose that they were playing some kind of celestial joke upon me, with merry incidental music from Gareth on his flute and Christopher upon his organ at St George's Hanover Square.

Ho, ho, ho! Happy Birthday, Bros!

The media are warming up for the Royal Wedding jamboree next weekend. While I rather like what little I know about Harry and Meghan, and wish them well, as a long-confirmed Welsh republican I cannot resist resurrecting two letters I wrote to *The Times* years ago concerning previous such goings-on. Here they are:

29 July 1981
Sir, I would like to put on record one citizen's sense of revulsion and foreboding at the ostentation, the extravagance and the sycophancy surrounding today's wedding of the heir to the British throne.

22 April 2011
Sir, At the time of the last royal wedding you kindly printed a letter from me complaining, as I remember it, about the preposterous flummery, extravagance and vulgarity of the event.

This time words fail me.

What shall I be writing next week? WATCH THIS SPACE!

In the welter of botanical encomia, popular at this time of year, glorifying the bluebell, the buttercup, the cowslip and the budding rose, I fail to find a single line or lyric in praise of the dandelion. Shakespeare, Keats, Wordsworth and even Rupert Brooke evidently ignored it. It was hardly worth noticing, it seems, at Gilbert White's Selborne, and the most interesting thing that William Rhind's *History of the Vegetable Kingdom* could say about it in 1856 was that older physicians recommended it in the treatment of hypochondria.

Well, as a loyal hypochondriac myself, here I am to stand up for this grand old botanical character, which for many centuries has provided food, medicine and arcane legend to peoples around the world. At one time of its life, when it is young, yellow and friendly, the dandelion sings a bold bass to the sweet contraltos and trebles of the cowslips and the primroses. Later, it veils itself in mystery, and the powder puffs of its virility are silently scattered across fields and gardens everywhere.

So there! Gardening snobs and ignoramuses may dismiss *Taraxacum officinale* as a mere vulgar weed, but I honour it as a heroic fellow citizen of the world, part dandy, part lion, part mystic and all jolly good fellow!

DAY 33

I hate to brag, but I cannot help thinking myself prescient with my comment on the engagement last year of Prince Harry and Meghan Markle – consummated the other day, as all the world knows, in a spectacularly publicized wedding. As a whole-hog Welsh republican, I had cynically sneered in the columns of *The Times* at two previous royal weddings (vulgar and sycophantic), but I rather liked the sound of Harry and Meghan, and when I heard of their engagement I wrote in my diary of the time that their example might 'conceivably persuade us cynics that family monarchy as a device of government is irrationally worth preserving'.

Well, we shall see, but at least I could tell readers of *The Times* in May 2018 that this latest royal wedding 'seemed to me a very wise delight'.

The most deceptive of the human faculties, I am beginning to think, is memory. We must nearly all find, I'm sure, that the older we get, the less reliable our memories are, but in many different aspects – forgetting names or forgetting faces, forgetting appointments sometimes, or even forgetting what we came upstairs for. In my own case, though, I am beginning to find that my memory is actually misleading, inaccurate, warped and sometimes harmlessly false.

I suppose it is partly the fault of my trade. All my life I have made professional use of my memory, using it, above all, as a chief instrument of what I presumptuously call, with a capital letter, my Art. It's not a very high-flown art, but it does depend largely upon the sounds and rhythms of words and sentences, which is why I like to read all my stuff aloud, preferably in my bath for resonance. And by the nature of things I suppose my memory instinctively moulds the nature and relevance of my recollections.

Could it be, I have begun to wonder this morning, that over the years this technique has been leading me towards untruths? A splendid old friend and contemporary of mine came to visit us yesterday, for the first time in many years. We soldiered together in the last days of the war and had ended up sharing a requisitioned house in Allied-occupied Venice. He was a professional soldier, born to it, and he went on to a distinguished career with his famous cavalry regiment. I was, then as now, at heart only a writer. How I enjoyed his company and his memories yesterday, after seventy years of friendship, but it dawned upon me, all the same, that our recollections of that distant Venice were different in kind.

Both our stories of recall were genuine, but they had been moulded and tempered, down the years, by the experiences of two different lifetimes, the very different lifetimes of two old friends, marching or stumbling our separate ways through time's tangle, and nurturing our memories accordingly.

A lovely day today, on a bank holiday weekend, so instead of taking my exercise up our leafy lane, I popped down to the waterfront for a brisk thousand paces along the promenade. It was exhilaratingly full of life – not crowded life exactly, but speckled life. Ours is a pebble beach, so there were no jam-packed sunseekers and sandcastlers, but clumps of people were scattered all across the foreshore, celebrating the sunshine in different ways. There were bathers, of course, and solitary scavengers I took to be fossil-hunters, and children at rock pools who were almost certainly looking for crabs, and lovers, of course, in the secluded lee of the promenade. Far away, almost out of sight, I could see bravos wading in twos and threes, and many dogs running towards the blue-green tide, and brilliantly across the whole waterscape a solitary windsurfer was storming and swishing and showing off his skills among the waves of the bay.

I thought it was all just wonderful, and to engage myself with that happy concourse I used a few brazen techniques that have served me well during a writer's lifetime. For instance, 'I could do that once,' I might like to remark of a child precariously wobbling along a parapet, and instantly I am *en rapport* with its parents – 'Couldn't we all! Those were the days!' Or if, passing a woman with an ice cream, I appeal that she give me a lick, we often end with her and her friends in hilarious comity.

And so on. The thing is that nearly all of us, old and young, on such a day, on such a beach, in such shared exhilaration, only want to be at one with the world, and welcome even the tiresome conversational devices of elderly literati.

A peculiar noise disturbed me this morning, a sort of insistent regular clicking somewhere or other in the house or yard. It made me fear that something was going wrong with the oil heating system, or the electrics, or the waterworks, or even with my venerable computer. But no, when I looked out of my downstairs window, this is what I saw:

Underneath a wooden table in the garden there crouched a ginger cat, an occasional visitor from a neighbouring household. It was not spitting or making that noise, though, just crouching and quivering there, but a foot or two out of its range, looking it straight in the eye and, yes, loudly and electrically clicking, a large, very handsome magpie was expressing its genetic opinions.

They were evidently not very liberal views, but felinophile that I am, I thought it had a point. That cat had no right to be there: that magpie's family had nested thereabouts for generations. I did not, of course, intervene, and left them at it, only relieved that there was nothing wrong with the lavatory system, and the last time I looked there was a sort of stand-off out there, the cat ostentatiously licking itself, the magpie withdrawn to a safe distance and rather morosely clicking.

They had evidently had enough silly quarrelling for the time being, so I suggested there was room enough in the garden for both of them, wished them good luck anyway and returned to my own footling preoccupations.

DAY 37

The literary people at the *New York Times*, who have been good to me for many years, last week invited me to review for them what sounded like a real blockbuster of historical scholarship. I could not face the task of reading it, let alone adequately reviewing it, and so gratefully declined the commission.

As I did so, though, it occurred to me that I have a book of my own coming out at just about the same time as that monumental work, so utterly its opposite in scale, scholarship and purpose as to be almost comical. If I am patently not of the calibre to review the one, I am certainly qualified, thought I, to review the other, so I wrote to the dear people at the *NYT* to suggest I review my own book instead.

They apparently thought not, although I assured them my self-critique would not merely be scrupulously fair, but might even be rather bitchily hostile to my own style – I do know my faults, you know. And the more I considered the matter, the more interesting I thought it would be if authors regularly wrote their own reviews – in tandem, perhaps, with independent critics, side by side on the book pages.

My own forthcoming volume, as it happens, is the first collection of the very same diary thoughts that you are reading now, and believe me, I am all too aware of its failings, besides being pleased with its successes. My amateur self-review would not necessarily be in riposte to the professional critique on the same page, and anyway, it might be fun for one and all to compare the two and spurn or buy the book in consequence.

But yes, it's true, I have to admit that when it comes to literary self-assessment my moral standards might sometimes slip. Like most writers (not all), I'm only human. That's evidently what the New York people thought, anyway, and they are no fools.

There was a programme on TV yesterday about the early years of the American space programme, when NASA had no commercial competitors and its heroes were nearly all military men. Tom Wolfe, in 1979, wrote a book about them called *The Right Stuff*, and for me the chief pleasure of yesterday's programme was meeting a few of them as they are now, when rocket flights to an international space station are commonplace and private capitalists plan tourism in space and colonial settlements on Mars.

Those first American space pioneers, though, really had to be heroes, and as one of their contemporaries, more or less, it was a delight to find them recognizably decent heroes still. It's nearly seventy years since I first stepped ashore in the United States, and one of the sadnesses of our times, to my mind, is the progressive disintegration of the American reputation since then.

There are reasons for it, God knows, but still I like to think that at the core of America – which is to my mind more than a mere nation, but a philosophical and artistic conception – the grandeur prevails. The idea of the Special Relationship between America and Britain, now in tatters, still means a lot to me, and as the poor old world stumbles on in chaos, it is a comfort to me to know that over there the right stuff is still around.

Being of simple tastes, I love a good tune, especially when it comes from the genius of a Bach, a Beethoven, a Mozart, a Wagner or a Puccini, and so carries with it the suggestion of immortality. But I enjoy a good contemporary show tune too, and one in particular has lately been in my head. It's called 'I Dips Me Lid', and I love it partly because it's very catchy and whistleable, but chiefly because it's overwhelmingly Australian.

I first heard it when I was working on a book about Sydney in the 1960s, and a hit show of the day down there was a musical called *The Sentimental Bloke*, with music by the Australian composer Albert Arlen and lyrics based upon a violently popular collection of poems by C. J. Dennis, who had died in 1938. My feelings about Australia were ambiguous – I had been singularly unpleasant about Sydney when I first got there, years before – but I did always enjoy the elemental side of Australian society, the raucousness and the merriment of it.

It has mostly been smoothed over now, as Australia becomes a mature and influential Power. It was still rampant then, though, and its old spirit is revived for me whenever I find myself whistling or humming a theme song of that old musical – 'I dips me lid to ya, sweet Doreen. I'll be your bloke if you want, Doreen.' It is hardly a subtle composition, but I like to think that it might easily please Mozart, Puccini or even old Wagner.

But by the 1990s, all the same, when I published my book at last, with the Bloke still in my mind, I often felt something more insidious about the Australian presence, more haunting, more subtle; and not having read my own words lately, I have just been looking them up, while Messrs Dennis and Arlen, out of the Australian past, still boisterously entertain me on the record player. These are the words I have found at the very end of my book, published in 1992 to a mixed reception, especially in Sydney:

> In the velvet sensual darkness on the harbour shore in Sydney, I sometimes feel myself haunted by a sense of loss, as though time is passing too fast, and frail black people are watching me out of the night somewhere, leaning on their spears . . .

O good on you, dear Australia, whatever you think of me. I dips me lid to ya out of your crude but lovable past, your complex presence and your surely noble future.

DAY 40

Of course I bow before talents and intuitions grander than my own – of course I do. If Shakespeare had written a soap opera, I would watch it awestruck by the range of his genius. I am, nevertheless, totally unconvinced by the purposes of the Bulgarian American artist Christo, whose latest offering, I gather, is a construction of 7,506 barrels to float horizontally upon the Serpentine in London throughout the summer, and to be named *The London Mastaba*, after an ancient Egyptian category of tomb.

Christo worked in collaboration with his wife, Jeanne-Claude – they were born on the same day in 1935 – until her death in 2009, and their joint output was colossal. I experienced some of it myself, and have never wavered in my judgement that much of it was perfectly nonsensical. It consisted chiefly of vast temporary transformations, sometimes in transparent wrappings, of entire existing constructions or landscapes, notably the Reichstag in Berlin, a twenty-four-mile-long strip of land in California, Central Park in New York, an even larger stack of oil barrels in the United Arab Emirates and a vast inflatable object in Germany which was lifted by two of the largest cranes in Europe, was visible from 25 kilometres away, lasted for ten hours and had, so far as I can make out, no discernible purpose whatsoever.

Well, the world disagreed with me. There was much, much more to marvel at. In Australia the couple were invited to wrap the entire shoreline of a bay at Sydney in synthetic fabric, and in Colorado $400,000 was spent on manufacturing 14,000 square metres of cloth to be hung on steel scales and supported by 29,000 tons of concrete across a valley in the Rocky Mountains (it lasted less than two days, before a gale blew it down . . .). The mayor of New York called the 7,000-odd saffron fabric 'gates' the couple erected all over Central Park 'one of the most exciting public art projects ever put on anywhere in the world', and everywhere administrations clamoured to be honoured by the possession of a work of art by Christo and Jeanne-Claude. Their wrapping jobs were, one eminent critic declared, 'revelation through concealment'.

The creators themselves were blameless. If they became rich by their creations, it was only, so to speak, indirectly – they generally financed their own projects and they never demanded entry fees. Their various purposes, they said, had no hidden meanings, but were simply intended to be beautiful in themselves, and to make people see familiar things in a new way.

Well and good. I believe them. I like the sound of them too, and I admire the colossal chutzpah of it all. But it still cuts no aesthetic ice with me. I believe the immense works of what their connoisseurs call Environmental Art to be virtuoso baloney and, having glimpsed it already for myself in New York and in Berlin, shall not be boarding a train from Wales to marvel at those floating barrels in the Serpentine.

As if they would care!

DAY 41

Last night before I went to sleep I finished my reading of Tolstoy's *Anna Karenina*, 960 pages of it, in the English translation by Louise and Aylmer Maude.

Long ago, in another copy, in a bar in Trieste and in an evidently tipsy scrawl, I scribbled the opinion that this was the best book I had ever read, and on the whole I think it still. Mind you, I strongly suspect that when I expressed that youthful and evidently inebriated critique, I had not actually read the book all the way through. I fear that like many another reader of *Anna Karenina*, the young Jan Morris had only got as far as Anna's heart-rending suicide (page 905 in my present edition). And in my opinion now, the best of the masterpiece was yet to come.

You will no doubt remember the young gentleman farmer Nicholas Levin, who has been a gentle, questioning presence throughout the book, but who in the end comes into his own as a symbolic master of final ceremonies. He it is who, alone beneath the stars of a Russian night sky, finds in the firmament some solution to the mass of problems, contradictions, mysteries and ironies which have challenged us during the long journey that is the reading of this marvellous work.

The simple power of goodness, Nicholas realizes, is the answer to those mighty conundrums – just that, however it is expressed or interpreted. And on the last page of my present copy of *Anna Karenina* I have signed off with no more than a grateful tick and the single word 'Kindness', which is how I myself prefer to interpret that message from the stars.

PS By the way, I see I wrote in that same volume, in 1999, that it's the last I could ever buy at James Armistead's famous Tillman Place Bookshop in San Francisco, because Mr Armistead was closing the store. He had written a farewell signature for me in the book too, together with a receipt for $22.79.

Rooting around the junk of my library this morning I came across a piece I wrote in 1973 for the London magazine *Encounter* (which was, as a matter of fact, though I didn't know it then, secretly subsidized by the CIA). It was a long essay about the British Royal Navy, which was for me a subject of profound romantic loyalty.

Reading the piece today, a generation later, has strangely moved me. The Navy means little to the British people now, and its very particular allure has long been forgotten, but perhaps you will allow me to quote the very ending of that old essay, for a glimpse of its meaning then.

It seems I had been loitering about the naval memorial on the Hoe at Plymouth, marvelling at its immense roster of fleets and far-flung battles, and its long, long lists of the dead down the generations. A group of chattering schoolchildren, with their teachers, then arrived in the little courtyard before the monument. At once (so I wrote) a silence fell upon them, and this is how I ended the piece:

They stood there not so much aghast as incredulous. The grandeur, the pathos, the scale, the sacrifice of it all seemed beyond their conception, as though they were memorials of another civilization that stood before them, commemorating the sailors of some foreign, half-forgotten country. Whose were those names? they seemed to be asking, as they stared silently at the slabs; and in my heightened mood of pity and exaltation I thought I heard a voice answer them out of the sea: 'They are your own, my children . . .'

Forty-five years on and I have questions of my own. What were those battles for? Who were the enemies? Why were they fighting? Why did they die? And whose voice was it, I wonder now, that called out of the sea that day?

DAY 43

Dear me, I hate even to think it, but is democracy past its sell-by date? In the dis-United States, in Atatürk's ex-libertarian Turkey, in Germany and Italy and Hungary and even dear France, nationalist bigots seem to be rampant. Above all in Britain, once the champion and standard-bearer of the ideology, the democratic ideal has apparently let us down. Faced with an ultimate challenge as serious in its kind as the Second World War itself, the British nation, in the early summer of 2018, flounders helpless and pathetic before the challenge not of a hostile power, but of democracy itself.

Not so long ago, its Government put before the people a simple democratic choice: did they or did they not wish to remain within the structure of kindred nations called the European Union? The people responded democratically. No, they declared, they did not, and so the retreat called Brexit plunged their once-splendid nation into ignominy.

I don't think we can deny the fact that democracy was the cause. So far as I know, the referendum was honest and straightforward, but we voters really had no idea what immense political and economic tangles would be involved in the withdrawal from Europe. Of course we didn't. We were simply invited to vote yes or no, and by a majority we voted no. It was a simple, genuinely democratic process, and it was disastrous.

Yesterday, I see from the news, thousands of people paraded through London demanding that whatever exit to the quagmire our democratically elected Government eventually proposes, it should be subject to –

To – to what? Why, to another referendum, that's what, five years on, by the same electorate, in the good old democratic way.

DAY 44

Alas, there is no denying that an unwelcome stranger has come to live with us at Trefan Morys. Dementia has latched on to my dear Elizabeth, and although much of the time she seems perfectly OK, in spasms it inevitably affects much of our daily lives – as it is plaguing the lives of countless ageing persons everywhere. It is horrible, but sometimes it has a laugh to it, and here's an example:

I was on the radio yesterday morning, talking about the lost British Empire, as is all too often my wont. Though I say it myself, the programme seemed entertaining and rather touching, and since it was to be repeated yesterday evening I thought Elizabeth would like to hear it. After supper, then, we settled on a sofa, switched the radio on and heard me perform. There was a selection of music in the performance, and the whole thing seemed to me quite enjoyable, so at the end of the half-hour I asked my dear old friend what she thought of it.

Well, it was all right, she thought. Went on a bit. Could have been better. And anyway, she added, who was that person talking?

Ah well, bless her heart, one has to laugh – *in dementia veritas*!

Snatches of Gossip

Yesterday our little town of Porthmadog, a couple of miles from our front door, was the hottest place in Britain! Can that be true? Of course it can – it was on the news – everyone is talking about it! It will make Porthmadog famous! Some people say it was the hottest place in Europe, if not the whole world!

And did you hear about poor Mrs B too? She's very poorly with her arthritis.

And talking of Porthmadog, I've been out in the sun leaf-
ing through an album of photographs of the town as it
was in its heyday, between the 1820s and the 1920s. It is
not one of your ancient Welsh towns, like Cricieth, still
closer to us, whose history and style are dominated by
the medieval castle above our bay. No, Porthmadog was
a creation of the worldwide Industrial Revolution, when
building materials were in universal demand and the simple slate quarries in the north Welsh mountains suddenly
became big business. Railways were built to serve them,
and a little coastal village nearby was transformed into a
thriving Welsh port, with its own shipyards and business
enterprises, its own particular Welsh society and its own
fleet of schooners to take high-class Welsh slate to the far
corners of the globe.

It is still a thriving little town, though the last ships
used its port in the 1980s and it is now dominated by
supermarkets, tourism, charity shops and Englishness.
Through the medium of those old pictures, though, I have
been trying to imagine myself living here four or five generations ago.

It looks to me, for a start, as though it must have been
a very assured little community. There is no suggestion of
doubt in these pictures. If I imagine myself a citizen of
Porthmadog in my great-grandfather's time, say, I think

I would have been full of zing. The faces of the boys and girls in the school photographs look at least as confident and cheerful as they do now, and the little town that awaited them in life was a hive of robust activity – very Welsh in style and language, but sturdily adapting to the demands of the time.

There was no unemployment, no cruel poverty, the chapels were full of believers, speculators and entrepreneurs thrived. Ambitious young seamen signed on at William Griffith's navigation school by the harbour, and on the floor below Mr Casson's bank had iron-barred windows, just in case. Mr Morris the chemist had two separate shops; a Pike family business ran Pike's newsagent in the High Street (and still does, actually, as was confirmed for me by the present incumbent this very morning). There was a civic brass band, and a town orchestra of some fifty elegantly hatted and suited performers, and football and cricket teams, and of course an enthusiastic local eisteddfod. If the fourth little girl from the left on the second row of the Tremadog Board school photograph, 1905, seems to be giggling rather too impertinently, I'm sure she was forgiven.

All in all, if I am to go by those old pictures, it looks a bold, confident, self-sufficient and enviable little community back there, so far from the centre of things, where a little society sure of its origins, its loyalties, its culture, its language and its abilities thrived before the deracinating world fell upon it.

Of course, there is much that is good still in Tremadog down the road, much kindness and decency; what is lost is

75

the creative buoyancy of identity that, just for a few generations, history allowed it.

DAY 47

Football has dominated almost everything in the last couple of days, because of the international World Cup contest going on in Russia and dominating TV screens from Moscow to Llanystumdwy, Wales, by way of Timbuktu. I have been watching it all half mesmerized, and it has implanted some new growths into my jumbled foliage of feelings concerning nationalism, patriotism, etc., so hang about, please, while I sort them out.

First, I am repelled, as I have always been, by the crazy flag-waving, chanting and general grotesquerie that characterizes the behaviour of crowds at international games of association football – soccer, that is, whose rules were first codified in Warwickshire, England, in 1863, and which is played, the rules say, 'by kicking a ball into the opponent's goal'.

Dear God, though, since 1863 it has evidently evolved in its upper grades, so to speak, into dizzy displays of skill and exhibitionism, that ball streaking madly here and there across the field, fought and slithered and tumbled for, projected by feet or heads, with virtuoso exhibitions of foresight and inexplicable whistle-blowings, and only very occasionally kicked into that opponent's goal. I hardly know what is going on, but I have to admit that at the World Cup tournament 2018, I have succumbed to football's fascination . . .

More to my point today, though, I have come to see soccer, in this its ultimate grade, as an instrument of good. Those vast, silly crowds, so far as I can see, are preposterously elated when their chosen team wins, but they do not seem embittered when it is beaten, and nor do the players themselves – down-hearted, perhaps, but not apparently vindictive. I take it that this is partly because soccer has become so truly internationalized. Professional players are swapped not just from team to team, but from country to country, so that local heroes are often not local at all, but for a transfer fee have come direct from Timbuktu Rovers, say, to Llanystumdwy Hotspurs, or vice versa.

And then again, and more importantly, the evil and preposterous prejudice of racism goes all to pot, if you are a football fan: for as far as I can see, every leading team in this great international tournament includes players of several colours, and in this, as in all else, their presence is merely a matter of common sense – or opportunism!

But most telling of all, I have come this week to recognize international football as a kind of universal solace. The world lacks comfort these days – lacks shelter, lacks certainties and loyalties, the props of religion and the reassurance of comradeship. In the vast, wildly enthusiastic crowds of the World Cup, during the last few days, I like to think I have been seeing the world itself enjoying, without always knowing it, the friendship and comfort of humanity itself.

A good American friend wrote to me the other day from New York, and for once in my life I disagreed with him. He was writing about the forthcoming visit to Britain of President Trump, and in particular about a wheeze that the president's critics here are preparing for his reception. Somebody has made a balloon caricature of him, a great big yellow smirking thing, nearly twenty feet tall, which portrays him as an angry nappied baby and is going to float over London during his stay – not in greeting nor even in joke, but obviously in blatant contempt.

My always fastidious New Yorker evidently approves of this gesture, and of course I understand why. My own ignorant view of Trump's presidency remains ambivalent, but I can well understand why every single American I know detests the man and his policies, and might easily approve of the baby balloon. I'm sure millions of Britons will approve of it too – the lord mayor of London himself has specifically given it his blessing. I am not, however, one of them.

I believe that civility should prevail in public as in private affairs – unless, of course, the preposterous primitivism of war intervenes. President Trump is coming to Britain at the invitation of our prime minister, our temporal chief citizen, and he is going to be received by Queen Elizabeth, the allegorical embodiment of our nation itself.

I am myself a republican Welsh separatist, but I can see the grace in all this, and I believe that kind manners should prevail between nations as between humans.

I told my old friend as much, and he replied compellingly. Good taste and decency had no meaning in the case, said he, because Trump himself disdained them, and mockery was the one valid tool to use against him. But he is a true American gentleman himself, and he ended his retort thus: 'If I cannot convince you, that's OK, because I will love you even more for standing up for what you believe is right.'

How would the president cope with that, I wonder?

DAY 49

Well, President Trump has come and gone from our shores, leaving behind the usual baffled responses! He behaved, during his few days here, outrageously and ingratiatingly, with clumsy grace and with crudity, like an oaf, like an adolescent, and all together with that mixture of the brash, the incredible, the inscrutable and the unforeseeable that makes him, one has to admit, much the most interesting of today's world leaders. Like him or loathe him, despise him or just throw up your hands in despair at his policies, there is no denying the fascination of Donald John Trump.

He is like some baffling missile from outer space, sweeping in and out of our terrestrial atmosphere and leaving chunks of radioactive substances lying around (his incongruously graceful First Lady fastidiously steps around them, and the various monarchs and lesser statesmen of his passing pretend not to notice . . .). As for me, I remain in hope. Trump has not come to Wales, and I remain aloof from the distasteful public receptions that thousands of English and Scottish protesters have given him. His racial policies sound detestable, his political methods dubious, but still I cannot help instinctively thinking that if President Trump's first incumbency has been a nightmare, his second four years may even yet prove his period of power to have been, on balance, a good deed in a very naughty world.

But don't listen to me. It may well be, as old Donald might say, Fake News.

DAY 50

Here's an astonishment. I was telling somebody yesterday about my dear Elizabeth's dementia – rightly or wrongly, I feel letting people know about it is best for us all – and he astonishingly replied, 'Oh yes, my cat's got it.'

Feline dementia! So it seems. The cat, having eaten a hearty meal, immediately demanded more, but when it was supplied, showed not the slightest interest in it. Dementia, was the perfectly serious diagnosis of my informant's vet – the animal was not, it seems, particularly greedy, but had totally forgotten that it had just eaten.

I told Elizabeth the tale, but she did not seem particularly interested, and as a matter of fact I couldn't quite remember myself whether it was nearly lunchtime then, or if we'd just had supper. Is dementia catching?

DAY 51

I generally buy our wine from the venerable, admirable and non-profit-making Wine Society, founded in 1874 as the International Exhibition Co-Operative Wine Society Limited, and still in its prime. Its enthralling catalogue turns up regularly and offers me a vast variety of wines from around the known world, all sure to be excellent, and to be delivered within a few days. What could be more convenient for a vinous pensioner like me?

And do I take advantage of it? Of course I don't. I simply can't be bothered. I just order the society's mixed dozens of whites and reds, just like that, taking no notice of vintages and such, and telling the society that if I'm not at home, would their delivery men kindly leave the stuff in the shed with the blue door in the yard.

And yet, and yet . . . Actually, I do have some pernickety wine preferences, to be mentally indulged with that catalogue when the order's gone. Sentimentally, I would really like always to have wines from places I know and love – Baccolo Appassimento, for instance, from the Veneto, its spicy character achieved, the catalogue tells me, by partial air-drying of the grapes, or a bottle of the Lebanon's celestial Château Musar, or a Shiraz from dear old Stellenbosch, or an honest Californian Zinfandel ('deliciously gluggable', says the catalogue), or something lovely from Down Under, or a bottle from the Three Choirs Vineyard in

Gloucestershire, which I always used to stop off at when I drove down from Wales to Oxford.

And then again, as a sucker for the crudest kinds of retsina, as drunk long ago in lively Greek taverns, I would be intrigued to try what is described as a completely new concept of the dear old stuff – 'delicate, fruity and herby'! Delicate? Fruity? Retsina? Wow!

Never mind. I'm just too lazy. The order's gone, anyway, and any day now those wine boxes will faithfully turn up from the International Exhibition folk, a dozen whites and a dozen reds, as per usual.

Micah the Prophet got it right! Who was Micah the Prophet, and what particular God or version of a God was he a prophet of? Search me, but today I came across this quotation from him, which I wish to endorse: 'What does the Lord require of you, but to do justice, and to love kindness, and to walk humbly with your God?'

Micah was dead right there, in my opinion, and it makes me wonder if he wasn't the same prophet, under a nom de plume perhaps, as the one who said to his audience somewhere else, apropos of an example of decent behaviour, 'Go, and do thou likewise.'

But does it matter anyway to what particular divinity, sub-divinity or heresy Micah owed his allegiance? I think not, and I think kindness is its own God, oblivious to period, creed, dogma or dispute.

Here endeth today's Lesson!

DAY 53

From my viewpoint, as an old observer far away in rural Wales, young urban England generally looks unlovely, ravaged and debased by the civic miseries of our time: by hooliganism and violence and racism, by obsessions with computers and mobile phones and reality TV and drugs and celebrity, by the general disintegration of family life and the nation's pitiful decline in its world status. From here, as I say, compared with how I remember it long ago young England seems decidedly unappealing.

Yesterday, though, I stopped off for coffee in our local equivalent of what the Americans used to call an ice-cream parlour, and there, as a lifelong professional busybody, I drew different conclusions. It was a half-term school holiday, and the place was chock-a-block full of families from our nearest English cities – Liverpool and Manchester, probably Birmingham too, big industrial cities which had spewed out their inhabitants for a trip to the rural seaside.

Well, I very soon concluded, young England wasn't so degenerate after all. I was hemmed in by it at my table there, deafened by the din of it all, slightly baffled by the jargon and the attitudes, but unarguably exhilarated. So these were the city children I had read about, the unfortunate young generation of Brexit Britain! They looked to me vivacious, amused, polite to the elderly and generally healthy. I greatly enjoyed the racket of that café, the racial variety and the vigour.

I am a professional instinctive (an abstract noun I have just invented, by the way), and wishful instinct rather than memory tells me that this noisy, undisciplined but lively young England is a lot more interesting than we were, when we were young and mobile-phoneless . . .

DAY 54

There's an old, old comedy on BBC TV which has lately been revived and caused some stir, because it was said to be perpetuating tired old patriotic emotions. It was called *Dad's Army*, and it was all about the volunteer part-time force called the Home Guard, which came into being in the Second World War and was manned chiefly by people too old for active service. The programme was, to my mind, endearingly and farcically funny.

I have some right to judge it because I am, I suppose, at ninety-one one of the Home Guard's few survivors. I was sixteen, going on seventeen, when I cut and ran from my boarding school and went home to Somerset to kill time more usefully before I could join the real army. I already had some vestigial military training in the school's Officer Training Corps, so I was welcomed when I turned up, slightly underage, at the local Home Guard station and offered to enlist.

The Home Guard was not in the least farcical like *Dad's Army*, but it was just as endearing. It had originally been called the Local Defence Volunteers, and it was rooted in its own patches of country. Most of our soldiers were veterans of the First World War, of all trades, professions and social backgrounds, and we were commanded by our local squire, himself a decorated lieutenant-colonel of 1914 vintage. We exercised once a week in quite vigorous infantry tactics, and we also, as I remember it, had our own cricket team. It was no joke. I have no doubt that if the Germans really had invaded, we would have been at least a nuisance to them.

Of course, I was a young romantic, and I can half remember to this day my adolescent emotions when I was posted with my ancient Lee-Enfield rifle to a hillside above the sea, looking across the Bristol Channel to the Welsh shore. 'Let 'em all come! We'll show them!' I probably said to myself . . .

But they never did come, and before long I went off to another five years of other sorts of soldiering, in other kinds of places, until one day I became another sort of person too.

PS I love *Dad's Army* still!

Today, a surreal transatlantic exchange!

1. I reported to an American couple that all the castles in Wales were floodlit because a Welsh cyclist had won the Tour de France.

2. She e-mailed her congratulations and added that she had dreamed we should all go to Istanbul.

3. Why Istanbul? I inquired.

4. She didn't know, she said.

5. I e-mailed, Istanbul, Istanbul. Why did Constantinople get the works?

6. He e-mailed that he remembered that song very well, and now he couldn't get it out of his head. Had I some remedial substitute?

7. I said, Try Beethoven's Fifth.

I haven't heard from them since.

DAY 56

Almost every day, it seems to me, the menace of Artificial Intelligence grows more menacing. Today we learn that a presidential occasion in Venezuela has been disrupted by an invasion of drones from neighbouring Colombia. It apparently did not succeed in its intentions, whatever they were, either because the drones simply blew up in mid-air or because they were shot down by Venezuelan snipers. Also, it is true, I suppose (I know nothing about these things), that they were ultimately controlled by human activists at Colombian bases. Nevertheless, yesterday the affairs of one nation were apparently disrupted by the actions of another, not by the use of simple rockets, let alone bombers or armies, but by the intervention of potentially autonomous machines, working for the moment in alliance with *Homo sapiens*.

It seems to me inevitable that such intelligent devices will, sooner or later, devise their own programmes, indulge their own prejudices, start their own wars, and that today's South American squabble is yet another ominous warning of, as the man put it long ago, Things to Come.

DAY 57

The milk had gone sour when I prepared breakfast this morning, the overnight weather having been thundery, so I jumped into the car and drove down to Cricieth to buy some more. It would only take a few exhilarating minutes, I told myself, as the old Honda and I raced down the empty morning roads, singing as we went, picked up the milk and whizzed home.

I was wrong. Hardly had we reached our own front door again than I heard on the car radio the opening notes of Rachmaninov's second piano concerto, and I was trapped in my seat. Few works of the classical repertoire grip me more easily than this much-beloved old workhorse of a piece, so variedly grand and wistful, disturbing and reassuring, patrician and populist. Rachmaninov's music was banned in Russia in the 1930s for representing the 'decadent attitude of the lower middle classes', and it's just right for me.

And glued in my seat there, the concerto also took me, in my traveller's romantic way, to a particular foreign place: the little Swiss town of Weggis, on Lake Lucerne, which we frequented for some years and which has left in my memory a marvellously jumbled mosaic of impressions: snowy mountains, placid Swiss waters, merry children and, above all, the comings and goings of lake steamers – graceful old white paddle boats with lordly captains and thumping antique engines . . .

Why do the emotions of the second piano concerto over-lap in my mind with the pulse of the steamboats? Because, as it happens, Rachmaninov retired to a white house on the Lucerne shore, just up the coast from Weggis, and I like to think that perhaps he too may have responded to the beat of those very same venerable pistons.

Anyway, I sat in my car until the last chords of the concerto, and only then took the milk in.

DAY 58

I don't how things are where you are, but here in north Wales, in a corner of Britain, on the edge of Europe, in the middle of what we used to call the Western world, if one is to go by the daily news, everything almost everywhere is in a state of muddled mayhem. Whom are we to believe, what do we aim for, why, or why not? It seems to me that the only people who know for certain what they want of the world are those with a dogma, and all too often, by the nature of things, they are dogmatic.

Too often the world's ancient religions offer us no alternative. You believe in your particular divinity, or you don't, and as a result millions of people everywhere have lost their inherited guides to conviction and behaviour, and millions more of us are searching for some new route to enlightenment.

Eastern mystics, although they so often mention a Way, are vague about a Destination, and Western theologians are more reticent than they used to be about the existence of an afterlife. Of course, they often remonstrate that when they talk of an afterlife, they mean something intangible, something merely ethereal, and anyway, I suspect few Western Christians, when they do something good, are consciously storing up credit for an entry pass to Heaven.

So? So I suspect – and hope! – that millions of us everywhere are reaching the conclusion that only one simple but tremendous conviction – Way and Destination all in one, as it were, with or without beliefs or disbeliefs – can offer us guidance through the endless tangle of the world's affairs. Tolstoy called it simply Goodness, and the intangible movement I myself have founded in its honour requires no membership, still less subscription, but only the intention of decency.

There! You thought I was going to say Kindness, but now and then I go in for Elegant Variation.

DAY 59

And speaking of variety, as I was in yesterday's entry, I note that it was the 250th day of this so-called diary, in its two volumes, and I am getting rather tired of me.

I dare say you are too, but then you can switch me off with the proverbial muttered curse and move on to pastures new. I am stuck with my tone of voice, the timbre and rhythm of it, the self-satisfaction and the sometimes tiresome humour.

More seriously, I am stuck with Me. For, of course, it is a carefully honed persona that I have been presenting to you these last 250 days. What a nice sort of person, I have evidently intended you to think, in the last years of a life so full of variety and surprise – sexually complex, sustained by a lifelong love of a partner, as of children and animals and home! But how often, if the truth be told, the whimsy masks bitter inadequacies, and how easily my vaunted devotion to the ideal of kindness fails me when it is truly challenged! I am not always as good to Elizabeth, in the growing confusions of her dementia, as I should be, or as generous to my children, or as responsive to old friends, or patient with fools, or, in short, anything like as agreeable as I have been implying for the past 250 days. And worst of all, perhaps, as I dare say you agree by now, the big doses of myself I have had to endure can be an awful bore . . .

But then again, come on, be fair, consider me now! How freely and frankly I am confessing my faults! I admit the worst in me. I apologize. Ah well, you may perhaps be thinking at this moment that on the whole this seems to be a fairly decent person after all; and may God forgive me, to tell you the truth that's just what I'm thinking too . . .

PS It isn't the 250th day of the diary – it's only the 246th! Watch this space . . .

DAY 60

This year the peripatetic Welsh National Eisteddfod, commonly touted as Europe's greatest arts festival, is being held in Cardiff, the national capital of our bilingual society. Very proper, you may think. Cardiff is the one great city of the little nation, big, rich, cosmopolitan, multiracial, historically significant and artistically progressive. Unfortunately, though, it is by no means representative of what one might call the mainland of the eisteddfod.

For one thing, it is geographically unrepresentative. Some 150 miles separate Cardiff, on the southern coast of Wales, from the tip of Anglesey in the north, and most of the country in between is profoundly rural or wild. Also, it is essentially a city of the world, an industrial, worldly seaport, experienced and outgoing, whereas the very nature of Wales as a whole is introspective, traditional, nostalgic and imaginative. Cardiff mostly speaks English, rather than Welsh: the Eisteddfod Genedlaethol Cymru is a festival devoted to the minority language of Cymraeg, and is famously rich in arcane ritual and tradition. Pitching its tents amidst the twenty-first-century urbanities of Caerdydd seemed to some of us anomalous and unpromising.

We were wrong. I did not myself travel the 118 miles from our home in Llanystumdwy to the festival site, but I watched it assiduously on television, and day by day it grew upon me that every now and then a National Eisteddfod in Cardiff might be a shot in the arm to the old country. It was sad in a way to watch those peculiar rituals being performed within buildings, rather than in tents or the open air, but it was fine to see unprecedented crowds attending them – 60,000 people and more – and perhaps experiencing for the first time something of the larger Welsh meaning. The language differences did not seem a hindrance – translations were always available – and, above all, the atmosphere seemed to be enthusiastic – not just the enthusiasm of mature traditionalists, but of an audience of all ages enjoying themselves.

For most of them, I suppose, it was an experience that was truly part of their own heritage, whether they spoke Welsh or not and had perhaps never set foot in the north of their country. Most of them, I do not doubt, were proud of their Welshness anyway, and pleased that this ancient demonstration of themselves, so to speak, had come to their own capital at last. I was pleased, too, as a patriot with a decidedly imperfect command of my own language but as an ardent believer in its prosperity.

Does a nation and its traditions necessarily depend upon a language? The National Eisteddfod is, of course, entirely devoted to Cymraeg and, above all, to its poetry; but there are many proud Welsh people who are devoted to the language but sometimes prefer, for one reason or another, to express themselves in English – many poets, for instance, from George Herbert and Henry Vaughan down to R. S. Thomas and that archetypical modern Welshman, Dylan Thomas.

Anyway, at Cardiff (Caerdydd) the other day I'm sure everyone sang with equal enthusiasm the first line of the national anthem, '*Mae hen wlad fy nhadau yn annwyl i mi*' ('The old land of my fathers is dear to me'), and its codicil, '*O bydded i'r heniaith barhau*' ('Long live the old language!')

And so say all of us, but to stress rather than weaken the point, there are people who are devoted less to the lovely language of Wales than to the still lovelier numen of the place, in whatever language it expresses itself – or even more persuasively, perhaps, in no language at all.

DAY 61

Doesn't regret nag at one? I was awake half the night regretting something I wrote in the previous batch of these diaries, which comes out very soon in book form, and of which an advance copy has just reached me.

In it I have mentioned my eldest son Mark, who has lived in Canada for many years, is a distinguished musicologist and has written, among much else, a wonderfully learned and much-admired book about twentieth-century composers. Well, in a diary entry about something else I referred to him, and when I re-read the entry yesterday, it seemed to me that I had expressed myself very badly in it, unintentionally seeming to slight his work and failing to articulate my lifelong admiration for him.

Of course, I did not mean it at all, but if that book is reaching him this morning too, forgive me my ham-handedness, dear Mark, accept my regret and let me sleep tonight. Thank you!

DAY 62

Every morning, just to make sure my e-mails are working, I send myself a mystic message on the Web, and today the message was this:

> muddle-morning.

Cryptic, but true. Among the myriad symptoms of my old age, two are now particularly intrusive: physically, lack of balance; mentally, muddle.

What an admirable word it is, by the way, wonderfully expressive of my condition. What day is today anyway? Who's coming this morning, if anybody? Isn't it somebody's birthday? Have I got to be somewhere, and if so, where?

Muddle-morning indeed! (And look back at my Day 59 for confirmation!)

DAY 63

It was my Elizabeth's birthday yesterday, and I was the skeleton at the feast.

It really was an excellent feast, too, with a highly cosmopolitan menu and a merry complement of celebrants, young and old. It all went with a swing, so why did I sit there apparently morose? I loved everyone there, but I am just no good at such festivities, and simply cannot bring myself to contribute publicly to the goings-on. In particular – I cannot deny it – I loathe the jingle 'Happy Birthday to You', with its attendant chorus.

I think I heard it for the first time when I sailed as a lecturer on a cruise ship long years ago. At dinnertime during that otherwise agreeable voyage, first one table of passengers, then another, often a third, broke into that wretched hymn to celebrate a birthday among them, until its cadences were stamped once and for all upon my psyche.

Where they linger to this day, and emerged at Elizabeth's birthday celebration, when somebody or other chose to resurrect them, and left me sitting there in morose and resentful silence. I need hardly tell you, I hope, that Elizabeth did not complain – after the best part of a century she knows my sentiments well enough, and does not invariably know what is going on anyway, so in fact I think it is perfectly possible that she actually joined in the dread chorus herself . . .

Well, why not, dear old friend? I sing it too, in my heart!

DAY 64

Aha! Just for once, an entirely happy story in the day's news. It concerns the astrophysicist Jocelyn Bell Burnell, who as a postgraduate student scientist at Cambridge in 1967 discovered the existence of pulsars. Her supervisor at the Cavendish Laboratory corroborated the work, and he alone it was who was awarded the Nobel Prize for the epochal achievement.

Eminent scientists, I gather, protested at the unfairness of this, but young Ms Burnell, then in her thirties, accepted the situation without complaint, and just went on with her work.

Which led her, this week, to America, and the award of something called the Special Breakthrough Prize, which is awarded for exceptional scientific achievement anywhere in the world and is worth – wait for it! – £2.3 million.

And how did Burnell, now in her seventies and a tremendously eminent Dame of the British Empire, respond this time? Why, by gracefully refusing that fortune for herself, and passing the whole lot to a scientific charity.

Bravo! Congratulations from a total scientific ignoramus, Dame Jocelyn, and thanks a lot for the example to us all.

DAY 65

I'm big on goats, who will one day, I suspect, inherit the earth from us, and when I found in a tourist brochure yesterday that a sort of entertainment ranch near us went in for pygmy goats, my heart leapt. Pygmy goats! I had never heard of such creatures, and could hardly imagine anything more desirable. A cuddly, sweet version of horny old Capricorn, ready to snuggle up with me at bedtime in lieu of my dear friend, the late Norwegian cat Ibsen!

But 'Huh!' in my mind I heard old Ibsen snarl. 'And just when did I ever snuggle up with you? Dear God, snuggling is hardly my style, and I think you'll find that Capricorn feels likewise.'

This morning I drove over to that farm anyway. There were baby rabbits to be handled there, and lambs, and baby guinea pigs, nice little ponies and adorable kittens somewhere, I don't doubt. But the pygmy goats seemed to me not sweetly pygmean at all. Tough, determined animals they turned out to be as they jostled around the bag of victuals I had brought for them, handsomely horned and bearded and full of grasping, greedy vigour.

'What did I tell you?' Ibsen murmured in my mind's ear. 'Try cuddling one of those little bruisers.' I threw the rest of the victuals over the fence for them to fight over, and went home with my old respect for Capricorn confirmed.

So the cat was right.

DAY 66

Among the delights of living in Welsh Wales, in one of those parts of the little country that has not been deracinated by tourism and second homes, is the sense of an age-old Instinct, working away beneath the surface of things, according to its own values, with its own meanings.

My poet son Twm inhabits that other Instinct. He lives and writes anyway in the Welsh language, but I often feel that his love for Wales, which of course I share, shimmers more subtly somehow, on another wavelength from mine. Of course, it is partly because his command of the language is infinitely more absolute than mine, but it is chiefly because he is a member of the Instinct.

Every now and then he is asked, by a neighbour, a friend, an acquaintance or even a total stranger, to write a poem in perfect literary Welsh to be read at somebody's funeral (or wedding, or birthday, or celebration of retirement). So natural is that sense of innate comradeship that on the one side the bereaved or celebrant simply asks, on the other the poet sings.

The tourists flock to the beach, the retirees watch their televisions, and they will seldom know of that lovely Instinct all around . . .

DAY 67

Once again, and surely for the last time, as I approach my ninety-second birthday I am thrust, almost detonated into a relative limelight. This is because the previous volume of these modest meditations has just been published, and to a degree unexampled in my own career, has been publicized! Times have changed in the literary industry, and while the most I used to get when a new book came out was a modest launch party, perhaps, and possibly an ad in one of the literary magazines, this time, my goodness, it feels positively explosive!

Somebody got the book on the radio, for a start, so that for a whole week extracts were broadcast. Then there was a small spate of interviews, when kindly, inquisitive journalists came to inspect the Morris ménage and incidentally mentioned the book. And the volume's own publishers, Faber & Faber, my benefactors for half a century, broke with old styles by distributing an extraordinary sort of publicity portfolio, including tea cloths with quotes from the book on them and a clothes line to dry them from, with pegs.

And it worked, my goodness it worked! I don't know if it sold many books, but to judge from my letters, e-mails and phone calls it made me famous for a whole week, largely, I suspect, among people who did not realize I was still alive.

Well, I was, and still am. Who d'you suppose is writing this, and why?

DAY 68

My heart leapt this morning when I read about the prime minister of New Zealand taking her baby with her to a session of the United Nations General Assembly. In my ignorance I had never heard of the lady before, but I liked the sound of her at once. Her name, I discovered as I read on, is Jacinda Ardern, and her policies in general seem liberal and generous, inasmuch as my ten minutes' reading persuades me. But it was not the baby bit, nor yet the ideology that excited me just now. It was this: that for the very, very first time in my life I read of a politician employing as a plank in their policies the conception of Kindness.

Well, have you ever heard a politician even *use* the word? Yet Kindness is, to my mind, as loyalties of all sorts lose their magnetism, the one abstract conception that might persuade us all of our fundamental human unity. I am not in the least ashamed of plugging it as a substitute for political systems, and indeed when years ago I half seriously proposed to found the Party of Kindness, many of my readers wanted to join it.

But no. Only Prime Minister Ardern, so far as I know, has shown any sign of thinking of Kindness as a political factor. I may have misunderstood her too, but anyway, the baby's welcome to the General Assembly seemed a start.

DAY 69

Like most of us, I fear, I have sort of given up on Brexit. 'For Heaven's sake,' I hear the poor old nation murmuring with me to its wretched politicians, 'get on with it, stop squabbling, reach some damned conclusion or other – by now we don't much care what conclusion it is anyway.'

But if it's a political quagmire over here, in the autumn of 2018, my mind boggles at the news that daily emanates from Washington DC. I read about it dutifully time and again, but still cannot distinguish a Blasey Ford from a Chuck Schumer or, for that matter, from a Chuck Grassley, identify Deborah Ramirez as against Susan Collins, or even remember for sure who is a Democrat and who a Republican. I read yesterday that Mitch McConnell (Democrat? Republican? Search me) proposed a closure vote to end the debate on Kavanaugh's nomination today, but shame on me, I have quite forgotten who Kavanaugh is, what he is being nominated for or what a closure vote is when it's at home (if you will pardon the vernacular).

It is almost a relief to turn to the news about President Trump, whose appeal to old-fashioned patriotism may be deceptive but is at least comprehensible . . . And anyway, by the time you read this, history itself will have moved on, rather out of breath, I would imagine.

DAY 70

Don't you ever feel that Nature itself is stacked against us in conspiracy? I felt downright resentful today when it seemed to intervene in my daily physical enterprise – the thousand paces along our lane, which I think of as a sort of spiritual exercise too. It was a boisterous morning, with a fierce north wind blustering directly into my face down the line of the lane, and I took this as a cheerful challenge.

My marching phrase of the day was, 'I'm old-fashioned, and I don't mind it, so long as you'll agree to stay old-fashioned with me,' and I dedicated it to the North Wind as I hummed it in my mind. If Nature played fair with me, I would respect its grandeur in return, and after all, I reasoned, when I turned back at the end of the lane the good old wind would be merrily helping me home!

But did it? Did it hell! Nature at that very moment decided to give the North Wind a rest and release the South Wind from its restraints. Fiercely, reproachfully, resentfully, this unpleasant zephyr howled directly up the line of my walk into my poor old nonagenarian face, and as I struggled home I shouted out loud, believe me, a very different ditty.

PS Yes, I know, I know, a zephyr is a west wind, but I like the word, and I've never had a chance to use it before.

I'm always disappointed when people don't notice my
dark blue blazer, which is one of a kind, and which I am
always eager to elucidate. As a blazer it is nothing extraordinary, but on it there are two quite different badges, and
as I am longing to tell you now, only two people in the
world are qualified to wear both of them. One is the friend
who years ago gave me the blazer as a Christmas present.
The other is me.

Everyone – well, come on, nearly everyone – knows the
badge on my left breast. It is the crest of Christ Church
College at the University of Oxford, ancient, grand,
proud, founded by Cardinal Wolsey in 1525, where thir-
teen prime ministers of England have been educated, not
to mention Lewis Carroll, King Edward VII, John Locke,
W. H. Auden, John Ruskin, William Walton and a thousand assorted divines. The Christ Church insignia, with
its tasselled cardinal's hat, must be one of the best known
of all academic totems, and I am proud myself of having
been a member of the House, as we call it, from 1936, when
I became a child chorister there, and from 1945, when I
was an undergraduate there, to this very day, when I am
an Honorary Student (i.e. Fellow) of the place.

But to my mind my other badge is just as appealing, and
more subtle in its appeal for me. It is the regimental crest of
the 9th Queen's Royal Lancers of the British Army, born

as Wynne's Dragoons in 1715, and proudly active through countless campaigns until its loss of identity in 1960 – not for nothing was the regiment's Latin motto translated as 'We do not retreat'. I had the good luck to join this famous regiment in Italy just at the end of the Second World War. I went on to serve as its intelligence officer in the Middle East, and I loved it from the start.

Loved it? Yes. I loved its easy style, its grace, its humour and its sense of friendship and community among all ranks. As a very un-soldierly sort of subaltern I found myself oddly at ease in its company. After all, one 9th Lancers officer had taken his cello with him for a campaign in China in 1840, and another had not only discovered a species of Himalayan poppy, but had translated into idiomatic English the odes of Horace. My own first commanding officer came from one of the most delightfully unorthodox families in all Wales, whose members invented the sheepdog trial and brewed the first Welsh whisky, and one of whose patriarchs, a successful betting man, wrote his own gravestone epitaph thus: 'As to my latter end I go, To win my Jubilee, I bless the good horse, Bendigo, who built this tomb for me.'

All in all, this jumble of regimental traditions and suggestions was very much to my taste, and one of the most prized books in my library is the two-volume regimental history presented to me by the last commanding officer of the 9th Lancers when the regiment marched into extinction.

And that is why the only other living person, so far as I know, who has been both an officer of the 9th and a

member of the House gave me my blazer for Christmas,
and it's why I love to show off its twin badges.

DAY 72

Ha, ha!!! I laugh at the spectacle of myself today! It's a perfectly ghastly morning here, a howling hurricane wind shaking the old house, storm warnings on the radio, everything rattling and shaking, and outside our windows the trees madly toss. The sea is a grey and nasty smudge, and there is no sign of life out there, not even a huddled cow.

I am all alone, and it is time for me to take my daily exercise: my statutory thousand paces of brisk walk. I have never once failed in this discipline, not once. If I'm away from home, I've walked some other route, but always with the same obedience to rhythm and mental music.

And today? Today I survey the scene out there despairingly. Must I really go out into that maelstrom? Would the gods forgive me if just once, just this morning, I failed them? Would my cheerful whistle falter at last, and even 'Land of Hope and Glory' stumble? I was ninety-two years old last week, after all, so could I not be excused, just this miserable once? But no, I was not strong enough to go out, but not weak enough to give up, and so fell into compromise. Surely, I reasoned to myself, a thousand paces up the lane was no worthier than a thousand paces inside the house, and so I set about marching rhythmically around the densely cluttered two floors of Trefan Morys, Llanystumdwy, Wales.

At least it was funny! Round and about the sofas I whistled my way, never pausing, through and among the island bookcases, perilously up the spiral staircase and down the wooden one, left, right, left, right, knocking over a vase and a couple of standard lamps, making the portraits swing, never pausing, never missing a beat, counting the paces on my fingers and sometimes bursting into song, until at last, breathless but triumphant, I reached the millennium on my thumb.

'Snubs to you,' said I to the howling winds outside, and put the kettle on for coffee.

DAY 73

I bet none of you had a better tea than the one we have just enjoyed here at Trefan Morys at the end of the weekend. The weather is still foul, but the old Norwegian stove upstairs is well stacked up with wood, and I have to admit feeling rather smug when I thought of all the poor tourists in their cars labouring homewards through the wet dusk. We don't go in for nostalgic teas, mind you, no Rupert Brooke ten-to-three nostalgia here. The five o'clock menu we enjoyed today was more Browning in style, and here's what we consumed, in mixtures to personal taste:

1. Earl Grey Indian tea, with fresh milk.
2. Olive-oil breadsticks.
3. Fresh Welsh butter.
4. Welsh blackberry and apple jam.

Eaten at greedy leisure, but with napkins always at the ready, because the jam tends to run, and if you sit too close to the fire the butter melts. As Browning might have put it:

O to be at Trefan, now it's teatime there,
And who ever crunches breadstick
Finds that butter, unaware,
Is blending with the apple jam and mixing with the
*   milk*

To make a magic substance as evocative as silk,
While the kettle boils and the laughter rings
At Trefan now!

DAY 74

Rather less buoyant contemplations today. Some time ago, a particularly charming journalist came here from London to interview me. We had an agreeable lunch together, and I was grateful for almost everything he wrote. I was not grateful, however, for the particularly unflattering cartoon-style sketch which accompanied his piece, and which was somehow to be reproduced all over the place as a sort of documentary reference – there it would be glaring back at you, looking part ravaged, part decadent and altogether unappealing. I tried unsuccessfully to have it discarded everywhere, but no, there that image still remained on public view on the Web. One or two of my friends expressed their indignation, others rightly said it didn't much matter, and over the months I got used to it anyway, until . . .

Remember Wilde's story about the picture of Dorian Gray, in which the figure in a portrait hideously ages over time, while the subject himself remains unchanged? Well, the opposite is happening to me. My picture remains the same, me it is that changes! The darkly accusatory look in the newspaper cartoon, the faintly malignant suggestion, the dark marks under the eyes, the brooding stare – all is there in the life now, whenever I look in the mirror.

I can't remember how Wilde's parable ended – can you? – and I think on the whole I'd better not know!!

The old, lost British Empire is still in the news these days, as its varied critics and protagonists, most of them unborn when its final Last Post was sounded, continue to debate its memory.

I stand, an ancient memorialist of the phenomenon, athwart the arguments. The intellectual and artistic centrepiece of my life was the *Pax Britannica* trilogy, which was published in the 1970s. It was, above all, an aesthetic view of the British Empire. I recognized the arrogance of it all, the cruelty and the unfairness, but I responded to the beauty of the thing too, the pathos of its mixed intentions and genuinely useful achievements. My view of it, in short, was equivocal, and so it remains to this day.

All this has cropped up this morning because there has arrived through the post the latest edition of the Hong Kong annual report, which has been sent to me ever since I wrote about the old British colony in 1988. This year's edition is especially interesting because it commemorates the twentieth anniversary of Hong Kong's handover to the Chinese as a Special Administrative Region (HKSAR).

The volume looks as elegant as ever and contains the same sort of classified information – Structure and Development of the Economy (HK's stock market was the third largest in Asia in terms of market capitalization), Health (the number of patients waiting in HK for double-lung transplants stood at twenty), Transport (the HK railway system carried some 5.5 million passengers on average every day). The book's beautifully reproduced colour photographs illustrate, as always, Hong Kong's versatility in the arts and sports, portray varied important visitors and commemorate, as usual, the docking in the port of a spick-and-span grey warship, its crew parading, as crews of the Royal Navy have paraded here for generations, in immaculate discipline on its deck.

Since this is a twentieth-anniversary celebratory edition, the book's binding is more light-hearted than usual, picturing as it does scores of the citizenry enjoying life terrifically in the Special Administrative Region, but one thing in it did take me sentimentally aback. The warship that is pictured visiting the port, as warships of the Royal Navy have been fraternally visiting Hong Kong for generations, looks as smart and professional as ever, but does not fly the White Ensign. That's because it is not HMS *Queen Elizabeth* or *Ark Royal*, but the aircraft carrier *Liaoning* of the PLAN, the People's Liberation Army Navy, 43,000 tons and carrying some forty Chinese-built jet fighters and helicopters.

Her crews, by the way, were partly trained by experts not from the Royal Navy, as they once might have been, but from the Brazilian navy; and come to think of it, if you were a stranger thumbing through the Hong Kong annual report for the year 2017, you would hardly know that the British had ever been in Hong Kong at all!

I don't know about you, but as a matter of principle I won't expose myself to the awful phenomenon called reality TV, and except for the news there generally isn't much on the public channels to justify the TV licence. So when the other day, in the course of an interview, I was asked what were my favourite TV programmes, I had to admit that the only two I regularly looked forward to of an evening were both frankly vulgar.

The Irish *Mrs Brown's Boys* is a domestic comedy which indulges itself, non-stop, in bad language, sexual innuendo in several shades of subtlety and the crudest kind of humour, the whole presided over by an overwhelmingly comical male interpreter of Mrs Brown herself, knickers and all. It is so frank as to be innocent, and the whole is played with such gusto and self-amusement that it never fails to cheer me up.

My other favourite is a very different kind of entertainment. It is the American comedy *Two and a Half Men*, and it is really dedicated entirely to matters of sex, as experienced, exploited and confronted by a couple of young men. This protracted, farcical anecdote is too much, and too crude for me, and the only reason I watch the thing is the quality of its acting, which seems to me comedy performance of near perfection. I don't know if its two stars find the script itself very funny, which I generally don't, but I admire their professional techniques as I enjoy really polished Shakespearean acting.

So just those two programmes make my television licence worth paying for, whatever you may think of my taste (and actually, being so immensely old, I don't have to pay for it anyway).

Every year for many years I have received from America, out of the blue, the present of a curious and often beautiful *objet d'art*. Over time it has variously been, for example, a Japanese figurine with a music disc in its innards, a gracefully distorted *trompe l'oeil* china cup and saucer, a handsome doll's house, lavishly furnished and complete with catalogue, a musical box, a blanket, a cut-out figure of a scorpion and a wooden puzzle called a tangram, which took a year to make and in my experience at least another year to solve. All – and there have been many more of them – are original works of art, intriguing and delightful too.

Scores of this munificent Christmas box have doubtless been distributed to recipients around the world, and I like to think that our benefactor, whom I have never met, is himself a sort of model American. Is the company name Norton AntiVirus familiar to you? Well, Mr Norton is the liberal-minded, generous, imaginative, humorous and artistic capitalist who has been sending us these unique presents year after year out of the blue.

Today, at the start of 2019, there arrived a magnificently produced volume detailing in full colour the entire corpus of the enterprise. It was The End, it announced. There would be no more of our fascinating annual gifts. I have just played the musical box in grateful requiem, and this afternoon will have another go at the tangram.

DAY 78

Very often, for what it's worth, I compose these little diary entries in my mind during my morning exercise, and if the weather is particularly inviting, I do it down on the seaside promenade in Cricieth, where I am sure to meet people I know and swap pleasantries with. Today was a prime example.

The autumn sun was wonderfully invigorating, the breeze out of the Irish Sea was an inspiration in itself, and there were just enough people around to stimulate passing badinage. With almost the very first step I took, the first of my statutory thousand paces, a fine idea for the opening stanza of my day's work came into my mind. It was a merrily inspired opening, I thought, and I looked forward to reaching my thousandth pace, at the far end of the promenade, and going home to write it.

O dear! So bracing was that sea wind, so invigorating the exercise, so numerous the acquaintances I met and such fun their varied small talk that by the time I ended my walk, that wonderfully promising opening to my piece had gone completely out of my mind, and now that I am back at my desk I am left only with this less than brilliant Day 79. Forgive me!

DAY 79

A Christian fundamentalist called upon me today. Not a mere evangelist, or a Jehovah's Witness, or one of those general-purpose sectarians to whom I am always happy to present the simple agnostic commandment 'Be Kind'. No, this one was the real thing: the Virgin Birth, the Resurrection, the infallible scriptures, miracles, the Atonement, the Devil – all the fundamentals of fundamentalism were absolute facts to him, and there was no arrogance to his certainties. They were all historical truths, he assured me, and there was no point in debating them.

Nor was there. He was a most courteous young man, unquestioning, and his utter belief in his own convictions struck me as being beautiful in its own right. How can a simple agnostic, groping with endless doubts, argue with such certainties? I didn't try. His interpretation of Truth seemed a kindly sort of creed, and that's enough for me.

DAY 80

I don't like to swank, but I often do, and I am always proud of my contributions to the literature of Manhattan – two books of long ago about a city I have long loved. One was commissioned by the Port of New York Authority, was called *The Great Port* and was dedicated, as it were, to the seamanship of the city. The other evoked Manhattan's effervescent delight when the end of the Second World War brought back the American armies from their victories in Europe. This one I called *Manhattan '45*, because it sounded partly like a kind of gun and partly like champagne, and I like to think that both will be read, if only as curious mementos for NY aficionados, when I am long dead and gone.

The other day, though, I discovered a book about Manhattan that I had never heard of, by an author strange to me. It is called *The Long-Winded Lady*, its author was an Irish-American journalist named Maeve Brennan, who died in 1993, and it has made me very envious. I'll tell you why . . .

She wrote nearly all of it in instalments for the *New Yorker* in the 1960s, and immersed herself absolutely, issue after issue, in every aspect of the city's life. Now I don't for a moment claim that I could do the job as brilliantly as she did, but it does seem to me that she dealt with the endless spectacle of Manhattan in somewhat the same way as

I have been reflecting on life in a small Welsh neighbour-hood in these daily jottings.

Don't laugh! But think of the wealth of material Manhattan offered for her column, minutiae to grand slam, day after day, as she roamed that terrific metropolis! And compare it with my snatches of local gossip, or my own laboured thoughts during my thousand paces of exer-cise along our lane at Llanystumdwy!

Yes, I am green with envy of the Long-Winded Lady . . .

My dear Elizabeth, being under the weather, yesterday received the following get-well card from a granddaughter, ten years old this very day, passing on the advice of a benign elephant:

Elephant's a friend of mine. Elephant says, 'Get well, Nan,
Eat and drink as well as rest.'
Dr Elephant knows best.

He certainly seems to be an educated sort of pachyderm, doesn't he? Nevertheless, I am replying thus on the child's behalf:

Well, dear Dr Jumbo, of course it's nice to be told,
But I cannot resist retorting, if I may be so bold,
One needs no elementary advice when one is TEN YEARS OLD!

DAY 82

I would not wish to be a news editor today (assuming that such people still exist in this age of the blog, the tweet and social media). It would be like being flooded, I think, by a hot, stinking tide of events from every corner of the world (I nearly wrote 'the known world', but of course there is no *un*known corner of the world nowadays . . .).

Anyway, as I was saying, I would not like the job nowadays, when thousands of spectacularly newsworthy things are happening every day and everywhere. This very morning, for example, I find in my paper a veritable host of news items, each one of which might have been an excitement during my own time in the business: items about, for instance, alleged Russian interference in British politics, US sanctions upon Iran, lethal floods in Italy, votes against national independence in New Caledonia, opposition politicians jailed in Bahrain, Christian pilgrims killed in Egypt, wild boars scavenging in Barcelona and people-smuggling in Yemen. Most challenging of all, perhaps, for harassed subeditors might be the news that an American woman in the United States has been luring armed police to the homes of Asian families in Manchester, England, claiming that they are abusing children . . .

'OK, OK,' as they used to say in the newsrooms as they prepared to go home. 'That's enough, put the old lady to bed.'

DAY 83

Here's a lovely thing that has happened to me. When they made my first collection of these diary pieces into a book, I added a dedication, thus:

For
One and All
Kindlily
(and yes, there is such a word!)

Well, last night I went into town in a misty, rainy dusk to collect a load of firewood, and as I began to load it up a vague, burly figure emerged unexpectedly out of the half-light to carry it all to the car for me. I don't know who he was. I didn't recognize him – could hardly see him really – and when he finished the job he just melted into the mist again without a word. I called after him through the darkness to thank him for his great kindness, and after a pause his voice came back to me there.

'I try to behave kindlily,' it said, and then after another pause, more faintly still:

'And yes, there is such a word.'

Never in half a century of the writing life have I been so delightfully quoted.

On Idyllism

When people ask me how to get to our house, I tell them
to come straight up the lane and through the farmyard,
and Trefan Morys is the house immediately on the right,
opposite the big elm, with the white cupola and weather-
vane on its roof. How idyllic it sounds, doesn't it, with the
farmyard and the elm? But I'll tell you what the farmyard
contains at this very moment, shall I? It's a bit muddy
and slippery today, but I'll pop out with my walking stick
and see.

Well, it's autumn grass-harvest time in twenty-first-
century Wales, and the yard is cluttered to every corner with the effluvia of twenty-first-century agriculture.
There are black canvas bags piled one on top of the other
full of silage, and there are sheds packed tight with hay
bales, and miscellaneous trailers and tractors all over the
place, and huge tanker trucks, and random varieties of
mechanism attached to one another, and the occasional
four-wheel quad bike blasting here and there. Where is
the idyllism? I might well wonder on behalf of our visitors, as I retreat on my stick to our garden gate opposite
the old elm.

Wait! Just as I get there one of those bikes, with a chug
of its engine and a squeak of its brakes, pulls up beside me,

and one of our lifelong friends and neighbours jumps off his saddle with a kind laugh to open the gate for me.

Idyllism: the peculiar nature of a scene or situation (*Oxford English Dictionary*).

DAY 85

I've always rather liked the word 'topsy-turvy', and for that matter the concept of it, and sometimes improbable topsy-turvydom certainly can be delightful. For instance, there could hardly be a more entertaining item of news than today's report that in the village of Llanrhaeadr-ym-Mochnant, not far from us, a gigantic bronze statue of a chorus girl, nine and a half tons of her, twenty-three feet tall, is at this very moment being completed by the ancient process (it says) of lost-wax casting. Surely nobody can complain about that kind of improbability?

It's a different matter, though, when topsy-turvydom seems to be taking over the human condition at large, and it feels to me that we are in that very state of mind this morning. Whoever we are, it seems, wherever we are, whatever our faith or political conviction, we simply don't know what is going on. The ramifications of economics as of diplomacy are beyond us; half of what we are told we don't believe and the other half we don't trust. And if some species of political messiah offers us salvation, well, Hitler did just that for the Germans long years ago, and men of his kind seem to be the chief candidates for succession now.

And yet, and yet, there are millions upon millions of decent people around the globe – in my opinion, far more good people than bad – a grand majority whose immense power lies latent, untapped in the governance of our affairs.

Topsy-turvynance *in excelsis*!

Thou shalt not kill; but need'st not strive
officiously to keep alive.

Who wrote that? Arthur Clough, in 1861, and the lines have come into my mind because of our kitchen clock. It is a dear old grandfather clock, put together a couple of centuries ago by a local craftsman, Mr John Parry of Tremadog, and ornamented with pastoral scenes of grazing sheep, blossoms, etc. I am very fond of it, but horologically it is past its best and is complemented by a severely functional modernist clock on the other side of the kitchen, governed by radio waves from its makers in Germany and almost alarmingly reliable.

Now I hate to report it, but last Saturday Mr John Parry of Tremadog's dear old timepiece somehow lost the movement of its hands and tells us the time no more. We must rely on that modernist miracle over there by the wash basin. And what shall we do, after all these years, with Mr John Parry of Tremadog's legacy?

Well, what does Clough tell us? One need not strive to keep alive, and indeed I shan't strive to get that old clock mended, because it will always be alive for me in another sense – in its ever-genial presence there, in the fond reminders it embodies, silently now but teeming with suggestion, and in the presence of Mr John Parry of

Tremadog himself, enjoying a rest after a long and useful lifetime.

No, I won't strive. Tick on, old friend, if only silently, and thanks a lot anyway.

DAY 87

This register of thoughts is becoming a register of epitaphs – yesterday my dear old kitchen clock, today the 41st president of the USA. I suppose it's inevitable, given my own time of life. Even my dear old Honda is booked in for a final assessment, and by the nature of things a sense of impending closure now begins to drift through Trefan Morys itself.

I particularly grieve, though, to say my formal farewells to President George Herbert Walker Bush, because although I never met him, we were contemporaries in more than one sense. We were almost the same age, the values he stood for were my values too, and the country he represented I loved and respected almost as my own. In the Cold War years of my own prime the so-called Special Relationship between Britain and America was no mere wishfulness, but was itself a kind of Great Power in an uncertain world, and Bush was its real president.

I shall be sneered at for saying it, but the values I respected in him were the traditional values of the American Gentleman, and alas they no longer govern his nation and so set some standard for the Western world. He was, everyone seems to agree, straight, frank, brave, kind and friendly – in short, gentlemanly American, and I wish to God he was with us still. Don't you?

DAY 88

Here's another confession – they crop up in my thinking now and then. The other day, you may remember, I applied a quotation from the poet Arthur Clough – 'Thou . . . need'st not strive officiously to keep alive' – to the condition of my dear old kitchen clock, which is patently on its last legs.

Well, I cheated you, sort of . . . I was really recalling those lines not in relation to a grandfather clock, but in relation to me. I can never quite remember whether I am ninety-two or ninety-three years old, but I was certainly born in 1926 and am, in my own opinion, well past my sell-by date. Affection and good manners, of course, require you to deny it, but I should know, and I assure you that if I were to kick the proverbial bucket when I finish this entry, it might be sad, but it would be logically sensible.

Admit it! There are too many old people in the world today, and as scientists and sociologists generally admit, the strain of it is as profoundly deleterious as climate change, so ominously threatening the human condition itself.

Of course, I am not advocating euthanasia. Of course, like that of nearly every other ninety-two/three-year-old, my death would be mourned. I am only stating as a fact that people are living too long in the world today, and the earth would be a better place if more of us left a bit earlier, including me. Of course, we must not kill, but officiousness should have no part in it – 'officiousness', an excellent word which means, the *OED* tells me, the assertion of authority in an annoying, domineering way, though the Americans put it better in *Webster's*, which suggests 'volunteering one's services when they are neither asked for nor needed'.

That's just my idle thought about it all – not asked for, I admit, and certainly not needed.

DAY 89

My admirable housemaster at Lancing College, eighty-odd years ago, used to play classical music for us on his gramophone in the evenings, and I have never forgotten one critical observation of his. 'The only thing wrong with Beethoven's symphonies', he told us one day, 'is that they don't know when to stop.'

Well, I was all of twelve years old then, and I admired him for an obviously cheeky opinion, such as schoolmasters, in my experience, did not often allow themselves to express. I could imagine his colleagues in the senior common room exclaiming, 'Really, Handford, is that the kind of thing you teach your chaps? About Beethoven?' Besides, I agreed with my housemaster. I thought then, and I think now, that some of Beethoven's majestic works really do go on too long, with their endless false endings and repetitive conclusions. There, too, I am still with the late Mr Handford, MA.

But, but . . . He was only a schoolmaster, after all, and I was only a child! Who were the two of us then, or since, to dispute the judgement of an immortal genius? I still think some of Beethoven's masterpieces drag on a bit, but dear God, whose artistic taste is likely to be superior, mine or his? Or even my excellent housemaster's?

O dear, it's almost Christmas again, looming with sham holly over the calendar and casting old curmudgeons like me into our usual foreboding. It's not that I begrudge family, friends and neighbours their festivities; it's just that I am simply not up to it, physically, mentally, temperamentally and, yes, morally. I am no good at Christmas.

It may be partly because during the formative years of my childhood, I was professionally engaged far from home. And this was because I was a boy chorister at the college of Christ Church, Oxford, whose chapel is also, as it historically happens, the cathedral of the Anglican diocese of Oxford. Don't ask me why – I've long ago forgotten. I only know that as a result, I spent a string of my childhood Christmases hard at it in choir stalls and practice rooms, rather than festively around a Yuletide conifer. (Yuletide? Yuletide – old Norse, they tell me, and who am I to doubt?)

Anyway, I have never for a moment regretted or resented my absence from the high jinks. On the contrary, those Christmases far from home amidst the dreaming spires have remained high points of my life's long memory. It is not just the simple holiness of them that delighted me then and warms me still; it was the grand artistic legend of it all, the beauty of the music and the touching tale, the dear old scholarly clergymen who, knowing us small choristers to be far from home and family, did their best to make it up for us with quaint games and small gifts.

In short, it was a glimpse of something beautiful in itself, beyond rituals or jollities around the Christmas tree. It was a distillation of goodness among beautiful buildings and kind strangers, and when, a few days later, I found myself at home among my dear family, I loved them all the more for that other world I had been visiting, and ate with greedy gratitude the plum cake they had saved for me.

DAY 91

There is no denying the onset of senility, whether you put it down to Alzheimer's or just plain old age, and Christmas 2018 has brought it home to me with a thud. I have progeny at large in several parts of the world, the eldest of them now pensionable themselves. More to the Christmassy point, I have many grandchildren of Yuletide age, and for the life of me I can't always remember their names. Isn't that awful? It's true that I hardly know many of them. True, too, that by the nature of things, probably most of them have nothing whatsoever in common with me. But so what? Those young or youngish persons, far away or down the road, share my blood, heritage and responsibility, and I am ashamed that sometimes I can't even name them . . .

But anyway, I've slipped a modest banknote into each of the young ones' Christmas cards, and I only hope I've got their names and addresses right.

DAY 92

Well, Christmas 2018 has come and gone, with its usual challenges and delights, and today is 1 January 2019, in all possibility my final New Year's Day, and Elizabeth's too. She ignores the fact and just soldiers on. I make the most of it.

Of course I exploit the experience of old age. It is grist for a writer's mill, and watching my own decline, making fun of it, exploring its ironies and its moments of beauty – all this helps to soften the undeniable tragedy of death, and partly compensates for its sadnesses. I am often comical in old age, and if other people kindly look the other way when I make some ridiculous error or perform some preposterous gaffe, I prefer to find it funny. I have been disgracefully self-centred all my life, and it's only proper nowadays that the joke's generally on me! But it's not a joke at all. Laughable though it may sometimes seem, the truth is, of course, that I am approaching one of the tremendous mysteries of existence, when I must say goodbye at last to my dear old partner – herself ahead of me in our explorations – to my children and all my friends, every one of whom I can now see, with my ancient mystic eyes, clambering somewhere behind me on the steep rocky track to Nowhere. Some of them are laughing, some are crying, but they are all coming my way too.

Keep smiling, anyway. It may not be to Nowhere at all! It may be to Angels and mercy and kindness and white wine, with toasted crumpets for tea. I do hope so, don't you? Keep in touch, anyway, and watch out for holes in the road!

There's a lot in the paper today about the idea of Frenchness, as embodied in the French language, once the lingua franca of a world empire, and still employed around the globe, it is alleged, as a post-imperial instrument of French supremacy and self-esteem. I have not heard of a parallel among the vociferous criticisms of the British imperial legacies, have you? Perhaps the spread of the English language has simply gone too far, so that generations now astir have simply forgotten its imperial pedigree. It is still an issue, though, here in Wales, where perhaps half a million people (I am guessing) habitually use their own ancient language, Cymraeg, beside a population of three million who use the tongue of their ancient conquerors, and all-too-immediate neighbours, the Anglo-Saxon English. The struggle for the survival of Cymraeg, a most beautiful and sophisticated medium, is still endemic here.

For myself, I long ago threw myself into its cause, in some ways still a struggle, in others heartily successful, and the immediate cause of my epiphany was this: sixty-odd years ago, when a campaign for the survival of the Welsh language had taken illegal routes, I was asked if we could give a temporary home to a young activist leader just released from jail. We lent him a flat on the top floor of our house, and so for a few weeks we were at the epicentre, as it were, of Welsh passion. Our guest upstairs was its charismatic talisman, a youth of great artistic talent who was to become celebrated as a singer, and who remains to this day an honoured champion of everything Welsh. We were enchanted and excited by his presence upstairs, and so it came about that I myself have remained, from that day to this, a devotee of his noble cause.

I wonder. Perhaps in centuries to come the two languages of Wales will coexist in happy equilibrium? I do hope so, but then I am at heart an Equilibrialist!

DAY 94

It's not often nowadays, in these generally laughless times, that in the daily course of events I am reduced – or elevated! – to absolute laughter, old-school farcical laughter. So I am happy to report that it happened to us yesterday, when Elizabeth and I went to do our mundane daily shopping, just for a change, a few miles up the road in a neighbouring village. A helpful acquaintance had asked me if we had tried the new café there, in the main street, the rather handsome small office building that used to be a bank? I didn't know about it, so we popped up there for a coffee when we were done with our shopping.

The bank turned out to have been enterprisingly converted, so that it still felt amusingly bankish, with a big, defunct safe in one corner and in another a curious sort of multi-storeyed mock office suite, made perhaps of canvas, and it was this eccentric construction that gave me my farcical delight this morning.

It had been taken over by very, very small children. There were probably only a few of them really, but so gloriously vigorous were they, so wildly did they dash and clamber in and out, up and down that peculiar edifice, sometimes sliding down its unstable steps, sometimes disappearing into its bowels, now here, now there, up and down, in and out, backwards or forwards, that the whole thing seemed to be quivering with the dream-like energy of it all.

We never discovered just who they were, or just what they were doing there, but we left them at it anyway, full blast. Part incredulous, part baffled, altogether delighted, digesting our excellent coffees and clutching our groceries we staggered home to normality, laughing all the way.

DAY 95

Never get old! Never have I felt its disadvantages more than I do this morning, when my computer system has not only gone wrong, but has brought home to me, over my breakfast, the absolute gulf that exists between me and the generations that have come after. For half the time we do not even speak the same language. Who is the Server, who declines to serve me on my screen this morning? What is the Fibre I must apparently upgrade to? My own grand-children are fluent in the vocabulary, and for that matter an all-embracing culture, which I have never mastered, and I am left floundering in search of a tutor who will come up to Trefan Morys this morning to guide me into elementary clarity (e.g. remind me what my password is, and what it's a password to, and who is Broadband).

He is very busy this morning, his answering machine tells me, and there is a waiting time of up to ten minutes to make an appointment. The wait will be extended, I'm sure, to at least half an hour of vapid recorded music, so I'll tell you what we'll do, you and I, if you care to join me. We'll say 'Go to hell' to the whole lot of them, the whole caboodle, the whole bloody world of this morning, and go for a merry walk in the rain.

DAY 96

A beloved friend of the Morris family was the horn player Dennis Brain, the most distinguished of his time, who was killed in a car crash in 1957 (he loved fast cars). I am often reminded of him, because his recording in particular of Mozart's fourth horn concerto is regularly broadcast, and seems to me quite ethereally beautiful. There are brilliant recordings by other artists too, but none of them seem to me to express quite the same suggestion of mingled poignancy and virtuosity. Somehow it all seems easier to today's horn players, and when I hear Brain's interpretation I am always reminded of the sadness of his early death.

He was my brother Gareth's closest friend and colleague, my mother wrote cadenzas for his concerto performances, he remains to this day a gentle presence in my mind, and I have sometimes wondered if the tragic circumstances of his death somehow made the beauty of his performances preternaturally more profound than the most brilliant interpretations of his successors. Well, yesterday it occurred to me to ask a wise musician of my acquaintance what she thought of this eerie notion. No, she thought, it was not divine intervention that so inspired Dennis Brain and made his playing of that concerto so poignantly different. It was merely the fact that his successors played horns equipped with a more modern system of valves than his was.

So. One need not make sacrifices to produce great art, but sometimes it evidently helps . . .

DAY 97

For only the second time in my life I have just made a financial investment. The first one was the purchase of some shares in Hong Kong, and it helped to keep me solvent for years. The new one is £100 in a cooperative to ensure the survival of our village pub, whose admirable proprietors (who also make excellent marmalade, by the way) are retiring. In villages all over Britain one sees old inns empty or boarded up, beaten by the onslaught of the cyber-culture, if that's what it is – you know what I mean, anyway. Here at Llanystumdwy, though, Y Plu – The Feathers – is determined to soldier on!

For yes, even here, in this far corner of a small, lovely country, we are embattled. The world is too much with us, even here. You would not know it, though. When I had dropped off my cheque for the pub investment, I drove up to the top of a nearby hill for a moment's contemplation. It was a lovely sunny day, and our local metropolis of Cricieth, population 1,800, lay there spread out as if in exhibition – so clean and brisk and timeless it looked, basking there in the sunshine beside the ocean, old in structure, young in style, crowned by its ancient castle, sheltered by the mountains of Snowdonia and gently lapped by the Irish Sea.

Don't you believe it, friend. The world is too much with Cricieth too. Its friendly old family High Street is invaded by charity shops and estate agents, and half those pleasant villas are the second homes of the English bourgeoisie or investment properties on the holiday market. There are no friendly banks in Cricieth now, with friendly local managers – they have been consolidated in more worldly vortexes – but there are three cosmopolitan supermarkets down there, almost cheek-by-jowl . . .

Cheer up, though! Ours is still a lovely little place, still full of good, kind Welsh people, still holding its own against the cyber-world and investing its modest wealth in The Feathers, and I myself am only halfway through the pot of marmalade its late proprietors sent me for Christmas. Yummy! (And yes, there is such a word.)

DAY 98

While the going is good I've been trying, unsuccessfully, to instil some order, or at least some sense of order, into the ghastly jumble of letters, pamphlets, cuttings, maps, memoranda, notebooks, proofs, illegible jottings and despairing scrawls that might, I suppose, in a more mature household be characterized as my Papers. I fear it all may be a miserable legacy for my poor executors, but in the meantime exploring the mess of it has revealed something of myself to me.

In particular, I find, buried in the confusion, phases of my past that I had forgotten all about. For example, how in my adolescence did I ever find the time, or the enthusiasm, to put together several stout loose-leaf volumes entitled, in very flowery pen and ink, STAMPIAU CYMRU – STAMPS OF WALES, and containing rank upon rank of postage stamps, used and unused, appertaining in some way to Wales? Lots of them were standard Post Office issue of the time, and most of them were only tangentially Stampiau Cymru at all. They were in my album solely because there was an incidental appearance on a stamp of a Welsh breed of cattle, or a Welsh sheepdog, or a goat, of course, or a Welsh bard in a series of Poets, or a Welsh composer among some Great Musicians (was Vaughan Williams really as Welsh as he sounded? I apparently gave him the benefit of the doubt . . .).

Or what about these other four enormous albums, grandly entitled, in even more stately felt-tipped penmanship:

A COLLECTION OF IMAGES OF
VENICE
FAMILIAR AND UNEXPECTED

I was nineteen when the British Army introduced me to Venice, and I was evidently hooked from the start, because this collection is a really stunning ragbag of every conceivable memento of the place, lovingly stuck in the several hundred pages of the Collection: picture postcards and scraps of manuscript and auction records and gallery reproductions and letters and receipts and snaps of cats and details of ferry boats and Heaven knows what else I preserved long ago as a first big memento of what was to prove a lifelong passion – Venezia!

And so, as I rummage among the piles, stacks and muddled reminders of my life, I come across a third and final aide-memoire, bringing my nostalgias up to date. It's that awful jumble itself. There is no fancy calligraphy to introduce it, only a single aerial photograph of a house, stuck in a cheap folder, but it means as much to me as those grander recollections ever could. For the house, you see, is Plas Trefan, Llanystumdwy, Wales, the home of my heart.

We do not live in it now, my Elizabeth and I, because when our family grew up, it was too big for us, but all we did was convert the old stables of the Plas, at the end of the drive, into the more modest Trefan Morys, where we have lived happily after. So it is Trefan in the abstract, so to speak, the Trefan that has been here for centuries that is honoured by my confusions. Here in our old age the home of our prime still smiles back at us: the old house itself in a multitude of photographs and drawings, and the mementos of visitors of all ages and many nationalities, scribbling their signatures, drawing their pictures, perpetuating their jokes and expressing their friendship down the generations, and I have responded, too, with a host of my own fondly amateurish sketches.

So there we are. Out of that desperate welter of muddled meanings I have extracted at least some pattern, for those three enthusiasms of long ago, remembered in those half-forgotten albums, live on to this day, as inspiring as ever! Beloved Wales, inspiring Venice, dear old Trefan – I love them still, all three of them, despite the unsortable, indescribable and indeed inconceivable debris of their legacies.

DAY 99

I asked a young acquaintance the other day what she planned for her future, and she replied at once that she wanted to be a news correspondent. I assumed she was talking cyber-talk, but even so I suspect she was thinking partly of the supreme interest, long ago, of my years as a foreign correspondent, which I all too often talk about.

I baulked in reply. By and large what a fascinating time we had of it, we wandering reporters, at large in the years before Isis and co. or poisoned doorknobs – years when we might have been arrested but probably not tortured, when diplomatic niceties were generally sustained, and for the time being, by and large, in one way or another the world's conflicts were at least comprehensible.

But just think what possible perils my dear young acquaintance would face now, in pursuit of just the same profession. I would lie sleepless in bed worrying about her, if she was out on the job in the maliciously hazy swamp that is today's historical arena. Will she pursue her ambition? Probably. Would I do the same, if I were young and ambitious today? Oh, I fear not – and frankly, my dear, 'fear' is the right word . . .

DAY 100

Dear God, another diurnal centenary! Is it possible? Is it desirable? The most disturbing thing about compiling a book in old age, I can tell you, is the audience it attracts. Most of the readers of this diary of mine are evidently old too, and write to me in kindly sympathy and understanding, when I would really prefer them to be half my age, at most, and write to me not as sympathetic confrères, but as amused, surprised or antagonized observers from other generations.

Well, there we are. That's the way it goes. Keep smiling, anyway!

'Since I can never see your face,' wrote the lyricist James Elroy Flecker, addressing a fellow poet a thousand years hence, 'and never shake you by the hand, I send my soul through time and space to greet you . . . you will understand . . .'

But will he understand? Flecker was writing in 1910, and as poets are inherently young, whatever their age, perhaps he felt that a confrère in 2910 would be young of heart and temperament too – he would understand!

I am also a poet of sorts, though, in 2019, and I have a feeling that the world is losing its poetry – its lyrical instinct, I mean, its sense of a Beyond. Into our own times, it seems to me, humanity has assumed the presence, variously imagined, of some other kind of existence, and our efforts to shake its hand have expressed themselves above all in beauty – the beauty of faith, wonder and mystery.

But as I read my newspaper this morning, I get the sense, for what it's worth, that humanity is hardening, and that even the poets, a thousand years from now, will have given up wondering.

Here's a touch of poignancy – sentimentality, if you prefer. Fifty years ago, I wrote a book evoking the city of New York at its climactic moment of success, when, at the very end of the Second World War, the first ship-load of American soldiers returned in triumph from their victories in Europe. They sailed into Manhattan, as it happened, on the iconic British liner *Queen Mary*, and I was touched by this conjunction. I loved the city and its meanings, I admired the ship and its heritage, and as a fervent Anglo-American, then and even now, I was proud of the moment's allegory. So I wrote a book about it called *Manhattan '45*, and I sadly dedicated it to four American soldiers who had died in action only a few days before the war ended.

As you can see, I was much moved by the human drama of it all, and I was grateful when the American publishers of my book, in New York themselves, gave it a photographic jacket which was wonderfully emotional and was later to become famous. You may know the picture. It showed an ecstatically celebrating Times Square, the emblematic heart of Manhattan, at that very same moment of victory and homecoming; and dominating it was a young American sailor who had evidently embraced a passing girl in the sheer rumbustious joy of the moment and given her a wholehearted and obviously irresistible kiss.

The picture became famous, and so did its anonymous sailor. They exactly illustrated the nature of my book and its intentions, and over the years I came to feel a true comradeship with that young seaman. I never met him, of course, until his death I never learnt his name, but I felt myself a real friend of his; and so it was that when I learnt from my newspaper this morning that he had left us, that delightfully impetuous young sailor on my long-ago book jacket, I had my moment of grateful poignancy.

PS His name was George Mendonsa, and he was ninety-five when he died. RIP.

Business people of all sorts get such a bad press these cyber-days that it is always agreeable to learn of benevolent examples. I thought it wonderful to read yesterday that the venture capitalist magnate Sir Michael Moritz and his wife were to be the new sponsors and financiers of the Booker Prize for literary fiction. Mind you, I don't myself approve of competitive prizes for writers (delighted though I was myself, long ago, when my one and only novel was shortlisted for the Booker – we writers are only human, after all . . .).

But I am biased in favour of Moritz anyway. He is a generous paragon of a capitalist Magnate. Born and bred in Wales, fostered like me at Christ Church, Oxford, living in San Francisco, he was a writer himself before Magnateness set in, and he has since then expressed the condition in vastly generous philanthropic gestures. I have never met him, nor understand the exact nature of his Magnitude. Because of our shared love of Wales, however, some time ago I plucked up the cheek to write and ask him if he would consider paying the housing tax of a small literary centre I am bequeathing my house to become, specifically for the benefit of Wales, when one of these days I kick the bucket.

Back came the instant response, from the distant halls of

plutocracy, from Silicon Valley, as it were, to Grub Street:

It would be a complete pleasure.

You see? And there's style for you, too!

DAY 104

It was a truly horrible day here yesterday – awesomely horrible, horrible as in unspeakable – and I had a mountain of mail to deal with. When elderly authors like me publish a new book, as I recently have, we get lots of kind mail about it, and I always feel it my duty, and my pleasure too, to thank their writers. This ghastly morning, as it happens, there were even more letters than usual. As I ripped open their envelopes, one by one, and composed a reply either for the post or for the computer, and as the wind rattled my windows and the grey rain poured down, I really felt rather pleased with myself, self-righteous, in fact, for behaving so punctiliously on such an awful day.

As this mood took over, I thought I would defy the weather for half an hour and treat myself to a coffee down in Cricieth. First, though, there was just one extremely long, particularly charming reader's letter to answer. So to cap my day's duty I sent its author a grateful reply by e-mail, meticulously, at a proper detailed length, correcting my errors and thanking her so much for liking my book. Then, fine, the old Honda ran me downtown for an agreeable post-duty break at the No. 46 Coffee Shop on the High Street. My job was done! The weather was still ghastly, it was true, the wind still howled, but the dear old Type R rumbled me cheerfully home again, and I returned to my library well content.

But another message awaited me on my computer screen. This is what it said: 'We have been unable to deliver your message. No mx record found for domain,' together with a few hundred words of cyber-gobbledegook. All my self-satisfaction instantly fizzled out, all my complacency was punctured . . . And do you know why it was? Because I had left out a single letter 'e' in the recipient's address. That's why! I must write that long, courteous, beautifully composed final letter all over again!

'To hell with it,' I swore, 'to hell with 'em all,' and I threw my damned book into the wastepaper basket. I decided never to write another one, to sell the house, civil-divorce Elizabeth, disinherit the family, scrap the old Honda (about time too) and emigrate to Patagonia to grow turnips for a living.

Well, no, I didn't really, but you will know what I mean. Thanks for your company anyway. Now I must get back to work . . .

DAY 105

A journalist is coming tomorrow to write an interview with me for the *New York Times*, and my publishers are naturally grateful for the publicity. So am I, of course, not least because that grand old paper has been good to me for many years. Usually on such occasions a photographer comes too, and after a restaurant lunch we come up to Trefan Morys, my eighteenth-century ex-stable homestead, for a camera session – the whole always a pleasant little event, I hope for us all.

This morning, though, I had doubts. Two very old ladies we are now, Elizabeth and I, living alone at Trefan Morys, and today it dawned upon me that the old place is decidedly, after a couple of hundred years, finally past its best. It really is an awful mess now – nightmarishly cluttered, run down, undusted, with miscellaneous chipped ornaments, unexplained bits and pieces, half-forgotten mementos, indecipherable scripts and lamps that don't work all over the place. There are ancient rugs to trip over (some with maps underneath them, to keep them flat), here a bust of the Buddha, there Queen Victoria, a model American train at the top of the stairs, and the whole constituting all in all, I suspect, a passable forecast of Chaos.

Even the kindest photographer, it seemed to me at breakfast today, could not make Trefan Morys 2019 look very appealing. I told the *Times* we'd stick to lunch at Dylan's by the sea.

All the same, this afternoon, over our tea (Earl Grey, with cream biscuits and strawberry jam), Elizabeth and I, as we munched, took stock of our surroundings, and once again, as always, thought to each other, well, it may be dingy, but what a fascinating structure we do inhabit, as it were, behind the scenes! Trefan Morys is really just one big sort of allegory, half overwhelmed with books that may look disordered but are lovingly arranged, and everywhere we contemplate there are interesting things to rediscover: letters tucked in volumes from a lifetime of the writing and wandering life; sketches of curious origin; stacks of gramophone records ancient and modern; portraits from several generations; reminders and mementos of two lifetimes and half a full century of mingled experience.

But no, the quality of suggestion is not photographical, and I look forward to our lunch with the *NYT*.

DAY 106

As you may have noticed, I am big on allegory, allegory big and small, and this morning it occurs to me that today, early in March 2019, we are one and all living inside an ultimate one. I see from the *Oxford Dictionary* that in 1382 Wyclif wrote of allegory as being a 'ghostly understanding', and that's the meaning I prefer for the word. I am beginning to feel, in a ghostly way, that we are approaching the end of all things.

In the UK it goes almost without saying that we are approaching the end of Britain, let alone England. Do you remember, not so long ago, what used to be called, at once in respect and revilement, 'the Establishment'? It was a misty and half-sinister entity, at once social, economic and intellectual, that was said to constitute an inner governing class in Britain. Like or loathe it, the Establishment seemed all-potent, pervading every aspect of life, and in those days still evidently so firm that nothing could budge it, not fascism or communism or liberal conviction.

Well, when you did last hear the name of the Establishment? It is shattered and lost, and to my mind with it has gone, for better or for worse, that ingrained sense of cohesion that gave the kingdom its sinewy confidence. Not long ago – remember? – Britain's position among the nations seemed to most of us irremovable. Now, citizens of the UK, I am told, are frequently emigrating to stabler countries

– Ireland, say, or Norway, or New Zealand – and the very idea of Great Britain is increasingly unconvincing.

Greater by far, though, and infinitely more suggestive, is the growing conviction that the world itself is coming to an end. It is not just creative fancy, this, not just the ghostly understanding that Wyclif (and I) have recognized. It is not even just conjecture, but scientific near-certainty, as the looming threats of climate change, poisonous contaminations, tidal withdrawals, terrorisms and threats of nuclear extermination circulate among . . . among . . . among . . . well, among people who know about these things, as against those of us who think they sense them.

It may be only a ghostly understanding, but in my book it's allegory.

DAY 107

Here's a smile to say goodnight. I was standing this afternoon on the waterfront down at Cricieth, surveying, as so often, the sea, the sunset and the little town around me. With me was a charming young American woman on her first visit to these parts. 'Tell me,' she said, pointing to our fourteenth-century castle on its commanding hill above the sea, hallowed to the memory of generations of Welsh kings, warriors and patriot heroes, 'tell me,' said she, 'is that new?'

'Not particularly,' I think I told her.

DAY 108

There is a word I think I shall adopt to express my general mood as the world, you and I lurch into the spring of 2019 – our general mood, I think you will agree, loitering somewhere between despair and resentment about the state of almost everything. In my whole life, during which as an all-too-prolific writer I must have used or misused several thousand words of the English language, I have never yet used the word 'mordant'. Perhaps I should? Is that the one I want?

No. 'Mordant', the *Compact Oxford Dictionary* tells me, means 'sharply sarcastic', which is not at all what I need. In its full, fifteen-volume version the *OED* goes further, adding references to the word meaning 'a petty spirit of detraction' and quoting the *Spectator*, 1854, as saying that Lord Salisbury was, as usual, very mordant in his tone towards Mr Gladstone.

I want none of these meanings for my word. What I feel the need for is an abstract noun that expresses some more general, perhaps more mystical and less bitter response to the human condition, and so I propose to invent the word 'mordancy'.

Of course, the multi-volume *OED* has got there first. It says there already is such a word, and defines mordancy as 'a petty spirit of detraction'. But that's not what I want at all. No, mordancy is defined, in the *Occasional Jan Morris*

Lexicon (2019), as 'a regretful but essentially kind-hearted conception of universal bewilderment'.

There! Mordancy. By all means use it yourselves!

DAY 109

There is no pretending that writing this daily diary is as easy as it used to be, if only because, as the years roll by, I have less to write about, and the affairs of the great world itself, viewed from my remote little watchtower, seem ever more squalidly repetitive. Nevertheless, as any diarist will confirm, I'm sure, keeping the diurnal memoir is an unfailing pleasure. The dullest day is enlivened for me when I sit down to write mine, and if it's not always much fun for you, the hapless reader of my prattle, well, tough!

I've got a whole bookcase of diary writings downstairs, from Pepys, of course, and sweet Francis Kilvert to George Orwell and Evelyn Waugh, and it seems to me that those chroniclers all got great pleasure from the practice, if only perhaps from the thought that in keeping journals they were writing future books.

Sometimes, though, like me, they got satisfaction from the maintenance of a discipline, and it seems that one such was Sir Walter Scott, that writer of mighty novels. One day in 1829 he failed to keep his diary for a couple of days, and so lost heart, he said, 'to make it up for many a month'.

I know how bad he felt, but anyway, nothing much happened to him for a time, and when he summoned up the resolve to start the diary again, he thought the hiatus months had been hardly worth writing about anyway.

But the peremptory satisfaction of Discipline prevailed with Sir Walter, as it does with me. 'Hang it!' he wrote. 'I hate to be beat, so here goes for better behaviour.' And he picked up his pen again, thought up an entry, just as I have now returned smugly to my computer screen, and so, like me again, basked in Order's Piety.

Half the world seems to be snarled up in the labyrinth that is Brexit, and from far and wide friends, acquaintances and just casual readers of mine send me their messages of sympathy for the appalling mess we British have got ourselves into – even the Scots and Welsh among us, who have always thought of ourselves as separate communities anyway. Nobody can escape the quagmire.

Except perhaps people like my dear old Elizabeth, who now half lives in the separate, cursed dominion of dementia. I remarked to her this morning, as I contemplated the day's televised complexities, that people of our age will never outlive the tangles of Brexit; but, bless her soul, she cheerfully told me she has never heard of it.

Brexit vs dementia. There is no denying that in my life now the temporal miseries of the one are as inescapable as the weird evils of the other. Between two harmless old souls like us who have lived together and loved one another for half a long lifetime, suddenly a strange curtain falls and a long, sweet relationship is ruptured, if only by petty irritations. And in our case at least, the worst of it is that I, the mere partner of the affliction, is the one more insidiously affected.

You have perhaps heard how trying it is to live with a dementia sufferer, however long and affectionate the acquaintance. I suppose most people generally manage well enough. They understand their partner's situation, do not blame them for it, and adjust their own behaviour accordingly. Some of us, though, fail in this response, and try as I may, I am all too often one of them, and so encounter the most truly insidious power of dementia: namely, that its effects can be transferable.

In moments of exasperation, when Elizabeth's behaviour can be most unconsciously irritating, I can be unforgivably cruel. I use words and phrases I despise, adopt rude attitudes that are not my own and think things I am ashamed to remember. It is a sort of momentary Satanic takeover, and as a lifelong agnostic, at such moments I do begin to suspect that while there may be no God, there surely must be, somewhere out there, a confoundedly cunning Devil . . .

Fortunately, my ugly spasm does not last, and Elizabeth does not seem to notice. So now, having knocked off this splurge of a confession for you, I'm remorsefully going to take her out to lunch. But when I ask her where she'd like to go, and she replies, as she invariably does, for the millionth time, that just this once I must make up her mind for her, why do I always have to ask? – when she says that yet again, then, I admit it, a small gleam of Satanism does flicker in my mind . . .

But with luck we shall enjoy the meal anyway.

DAY III

Today, at the very start of spring, when the daffodils are splurgeoning all over Trefan and All Fools' Day is with us, an old friend in America has sent me a comic cartoon cover from the *New Yorker*. It depicts an unfortunate squawking cuckoo apparently being spewed in and out on a spring from the clock face of Big Ben. Alas, it is no joke, because it exactly satirizes the situation we in Britain – even in Wales and Scotland – all find ourselves in this morning, as we haplessly follow the apparently endless mechanics of the Brexit negotiations, in and out, twist and turn, to be jolted back time and again into Big bloody Ben.

I suppose by now we must accept that we are at a nadir of our nation's history – within my own lifetime deposed from a glorious climax to ignominy, from colossal self-respect to an American cartoon of a cuckoo clock at Westminster. Who would have believed it possible when I was young? Dear God, what would our fathers have thought, let alone our Victorian grandpapas?

I asked my American friend not to rub it all in any deeper, and he kindly responded with some thoughts about President Trump.

DAY 112

Feeling in a rather embarrassingly hail-fellow-well-met sort of mood today, I set off on my statutory thousand-pace exercise along the seafront promenade with Mendelssohn's jolly 'Wedding March' as my mental theme. It goes with a swing from the start – does it not? – with 'Here comes the Bride', and I strode along to its rhythm, smiling ingratiatingly to one and all.

After a while, though, 'Here comes the Bride' began to pall, and I could not for the life of me remember what came next in that joyous ensemble. So being, as I confessed to you, in a tiresomely effusive frame of mind, as I strode on I accosted suitable pedestrians coming the other way, sang the first bit of the tune and asked in my best boisterous manner if they could tell me what came next. Their replies were sometimes just astonished by so queer an accost, sometimes slightly affronted, sometimes more or less incredulous, but generally speaking, I must say, gently amused. Only one middle-aged couple took me seriously, thought deeply and gave me, as I later found, the correct and complex musical answer (not unconnected with Wagner).

I hope I was polite and suitably grateful to all of them, but looking back at the episode now from the sedate seclusion of my library, I am not fond of myself. I don't much like people of the hail-fellow kind, especially when they're me.

A touch of farce on a bad day yesterday (for at this juncture in March 2019, you may remember if you're old enough, every day has been bad for almost everyone on earth). I had taken my dear old Honda Type R into a garage for what I fear must be its final cosmetic makeover. Mechanically, it is as fit as ever, but even I am a bit ashamed of its multitudinous scrapes, dents and rusted scars.

The obliging garage people lent me a quite nice little blue Citroën to be going on with, and since the morning, if nothing else, was quite pleasant, I decided to take Elizabeth to a botanic centre, a few miles up the road, where they serve decent coffee. I drove the little Citroën rather gingerly, strange and complicated as it was to me, but I made it to the coffee place happily enough and parked in the empty car park there.

Until we prepared to get out of the car and found – lo! – that we were locked inside it. No amount of pulling knobs, fiddling with levers or pressing buttons could open those doors for us, until at last another car turned up and a kindly couple, responding to our farcical gestures of despair, laughingly opened the doors from the outside.

Well, it would have been laughs all the way, if it had not been that when we had drunk our coffee and returned to the Citroën, no amount of pulling knobs, fiddling with levers or pressing buttons would make its engine start, and because we had only popped out for that coffee with a few coins, I had left at home in my handbag the name and address of the Citroën's garage owner. We went inside the garden centre again and had another coffee and another . . . We were stuck, were we not, two old ladies not knowing what to do, but gradually as time passed it all developed into comedy. Not only the staff of the place, but all the other customers chimed in too, offering advice, finding telephone numbers, suggesting names, asking questions, offering coffee; and when at last, by somebody's magical intervention, I don't know who, two mechanics from the Citroën's garage turned up, and with lengthy tinkerings and examinations at last made the engine start – well, by then, we were grateful friends with one and all, and before we drove off home, with the whole place still laughing, the people of the botanic centre gave us a coffee, with sandwiches too, on the house. I prayed to God as I cautiously drove the nice little car home, not at all sure what buttons or pedals to press, but by the time we had got safely back to Trefan, dear old Elizabeth had entirely forgotten the episode . . .

And now the rejuvenated Honda is home again too, and smiling all over its face.

I suppose half the world, this morning, is yearning for a Saviour, as mankind (and animal-kind too) stumbles on through the morass of miseries that engorges us one and all. Perhaps, in Britain anyway, we feel it most if we are very old and can remember this country's halcyon years after the Second World War, when we were basking still in the glow of victory and the hope of happiness. Of course, it was part illusion and we were very young, but it was not all fraud – from our prime part in the reborn United Nations to the visionary National Health Service, things really were looking up for Great Britain, and many of us, young and old, simpletons and sophisticates alike, felt we had been brought to this by a Saviour.

Well, you may sneer, but I wish we still had old Winston to steer us through. Nowadays he is often reviled as a crude nationalist warmonger, and of course he had his blind spots and fallible prejudices, but Churchill the imperialist it was who nevertheless could write, in the prime of the Raj, about the evil side of Empire, 'the foul path of imperialism' and its 'sordid appetites'. In short, he was an honest, cultured, artistic, frankly fallible, courageous, gifted and entertaining gentleman, and in the absence of any divine interventionist, it seems to me that an honest, cultured, artistic, frankly fallible, courageous, gifted and entertaining gent is just the messiah the poor British need today.

Any candidates in mind?

DAY 115

The first lambs of 2019 are emerging into the world, poor little devils. No wonder, having taken a look at the place, they so soon hurry back to their mums' udders.

DAY 116

Conscience, as the man said, makes cowards of us all, and it certainly makes a wimp of me.

I've been getting a great deal of mail lately, for one reason and another. The earlier volume of this diary was published, and lots and lots of people wrote letters or sent e-mails about it, and then many more wrote kindly about dementia, and ageing friends shared their emotions, and total strangers expressed their good wishes, and all in all, it seemed to me, half the world was getting in touch with me, morning after morning, and I was replying to them afternoon after afternoon, until the other day I switched off and replied to no more.

Conscience, my adviser, took note, and now I am beset by ineffectual pangs of remorse. Of course I know I should have replied to all those friendly messages, and of course I know that if I tried hard enough, I could probably find some of their addresses and write gratefully to them now, but no, I'm a wimp now, a whining wimp.

'Who asked them to write, anyway?' my rival advocate Beelzebub slyly suggests, and he does have a point, doesn't he? But 'Get thee behind me,' Conscience has summoned up the guts to retort, and at least I am sitting down now to compose this apologia . . .

I have never met the golfer Tiger Woods, and doubtless never shall, but I like him very much. Partly, of course, I admire him for his professional skills and tenacity, but chiefly I like him for himself. I like the style of him, and I very much like the fact that his very existence makes the whole wretched obsession with race seem absurd. When Woods raises his club to drive, surely only the very crudest of oafs could either thrill or shudder because of what colour he is. By and large, even the oafs seem to agree that in this case at least, a man's a man for all that.

Of course history and circumstance have fostered racial bigotry, and of course generations of American southerners and British imperialists were not responsible for their prejudices. There are plenty of ignorant bigots still around, though, to spout their unkind idiocies, and that's why Tiger Woods is the man for me!!

DAY 118

Well, Notre-Dame did not entirely burn down yesterday, but it very nearly did, and it has lost lots of its treasures. It is heartening that the whole world today seems to be rejoicing at the escape and mourning the damage that was done to the grand old structure (minus, of course, the usual scum of profiteers, publicity-seekers and social-media bores). Not everybody loves France or the French, not everyone has been to Paris, but to my mind what we are really all honouring now, anyway, is the beauty of a suggestion – not even a conviction, but an idea, or an instinct. Just for once we have responded to a universal mystic call, and if there is a God, he must surely be pleased that the numen of one of his myriad holy places has brought out the best in most of us. Amen!

Here's an odd little juxtaposition of memories for you, if you can be bothered to read it. A charming small boy came to Trefan Morys with his parents today, and pottering about the kitchen came across a blue china figure of a hen, apparently sitting on her eggs. He lifted her up, and I heard his laughing cry of discovery across the room – it was not eggs she was hatching, but cornflakes!

Instantly, I heard in my mind an echo from fifty or sixty years ago, when I was on a guided tour of the White House in Washington, and when I heard a similar cry of discovery from one of my fellow tourists. What she had found was on one of the plates in a cabinet of the presidential china. 'Just what I thought,' I heard her cry, then and in twisted echo again this morning, '– chipped!'

Chicken eggs and presidential crockery – tenuous but tenacious are the wisps of memory!

DAY 120

A cheerful-sounding phone call this morning from a dear old friend and contemporary, but as so often these days, the cheerfulness was disguised. She chatted a bit, as usual, of this and that, but gradually eased our talk around to her real news: that one more elderly friend of both of us had died in the night.

Believe me, when you get to my age, it is a regular tolling of the bell, and it probably makes many of us wonder if it is worth living so long – all too often we've outlived our usefulness, and even, in a way, our identities. But I've plugged this gloomy thought often enough in this diary, I know, and I here and now promise, before I go out for my day's exercise, that I won't once breathe the word 'euthanasia' again (even if I've spelt it right).

DAY 121

Easter morning 2019, and what do the world's headlines have for us on this day of happy celebration, a day to be shared by people of all religious faiths, or none at all, as a festival of holiday?

SRI LANKA EXPLOSIONS: AT LEAST 100 KILLED AND HUNDREDS INJURED IN THREE CHURCHES AND THREE HOTELS

That's what the news offers us this happy morn, and what more can I write? I can only add, with a bitter tinge of irony, that my Elizabeth was born and spent her happy childhood in Sri Lanka, in the days when it was British Ceylon . . . She is sitting now in the dappled sunshine of our garden, and has not taken in the ghastly Easter news from her birthplace.

I think I shall let it be, let it be . . .

'Let it be' were the last words of yesterday's diary entry, and in a very different context they shall be today's first. Yesterday I was sparing dear old Elizabeth some ghastly news; today I am recording my own reluctant recognition that I am simply not competent, in my ninety-third year, to keep up with or even understand the world's goings-on. The argot of the cyber-world is beyond me, and so are the complexities of world diplomacy, economics and skulduggery. What and who and where are the social-media pundits droning on about today – are they goodies or baddies, or just bores? Should I be concerned about the election in Venezuela? Where is Huawei, anyway? What is Netflix? I feel my very sensibilities are being hardened by the perpetual miseries of cruelties and famines and poverty and injustices, starving children, weeping mothers, homeless families and despairing old folk.

So, yes, today I shall let it all be. And tomorrow?

DAY 123

Here's an unnerving development to watch out for, if you are a writer like me and will one day reach a comparable age. I have developed an unhealthy addiction to reading my own books. Some I have entirely forgotten, some I admire and some I deplore, but there is no denying that I do enjoy the experience of encountering them again, like old acquaintances. The oldest among them is dated, I see, 1956, and is all about the USA; the latest is from 2018, and is all about me.

Some of them I know more or less by heart. Some, dear God, I wish I'd never thought of. But there we are, the rough with the smooth, and the rotten too!

The power of words enthrals me. I have never until today used the word 'Nadir', although I have often, so to speak, admired it from afar – its simple elegance, its restraint, the shape and sound of it, its echoes of classical Arabic as against its mundane and depressing Anglo-American equivalent, 'rock bottom'.

Well, this morning I reached my own Nadir. I needn't analyse the causes; take my word for it, never before in my conscious life has everything seemed so entirely dreadful as it did then, personally, socially, financially, mentally and imaginatively. It was a Nadirian day, one might say if there were such an adjective, which there is now.

But you never know, do you? I stumbled upon a wonderfully curative noun in the dictionary this afternoon, and it entered my mind like a charm: 'Elixir', another word I've never used before, and another concept from the distant Arabic. Elixir offered me in magical potion the very spirit of promise and recompense, and marvellously restored my spirits . . . Elixir! I relished its sound and its shape in my imagination at teatime, gratefully employ it now, and invent in its honour a second brand-new adjective of the day:

Elixirian.

There! Nadirian! Elixirian! Get thee behind me, rock bottom!

Today's mundane activities strike me as characteristic of an old writer's goings-on at the very start of the summer in Wales. They go like this:

Owls wake me, hooting insistently until dawn. From our terrace I see our first swallows of the season, but note there is still snow on Snowdon. At breakfast-time a solitary Typhoon fighter from the nearby RAF station sweeps low over us, ready no doubt to defend us from all evil, and I envy its pilot, as I always do.

The morning mail brings me a payment of royalties from the Chinese translation of a book I wrote in 1968, together with instructions about how to vote in the forthcoming European elections. One correspondent chides me for getting a quotation wrong, and a total stranger says he hopes he will not be intruding if he turns up at Trefan one morning next week just to say hullo.

During the morning a kind acquaintance knocks at the door with a pot of her excellent home-made marmalade, in just the consistency I prefer, and in the afternoon some terrific small relatives appear and play virtuoso ball games inside and outside the house. They talk to each other in Welsh that is far beyond my fading command of the language, but sympathetically translate for me when required. Cows come by for milking.

In fits and starts during the day I take my exercise

(today a thousand paces along the Cricieth waterfront), answer letters and telephone calls, write this diary entry, read my current quota of *War and Peace*, and in the calm of the evening, after a ready-cooked supermarket supper, Elizabeth and I switch listlessly from TV channel to TV channel in search of something appealing.

Before I go to bed, though, I go outside and look at the stars. They wish me their usual cool, kindly and unearthly goodnights, and so comfortingly end my day. It has passed on and off in gleams and lurches, laughs and disappointments and nothings in particular – one all-too-ordinary day, at the start of an elderly writer's summer in Wales, AD 2019.

A glorious day today, and the splendid old sycamore that presides over our yard and garden looks quite particularly benign and self-satisfied. I'm grateful to it, as always, because for me the pleasure of the plant life of our domain comes chiefly from its shades and contrasts.

The early-summer colours are lovely, of course – bright blues and yellows and pinks massed in banks and bushes, brazen in bold patches and shamelessly showing off their splendours down the banks of the lane. It is the inner suggestiveness of the scene, though, the hints and proposals and errors, that gives me my own magics, courtesy of that grand old sycamore.

For example, if you look through its shady lower branches, you will see far away, in distant sunshine, the suggestion of some other country altogether far, far away, where altogether foreign peoples must surely be living and loving, with hybrid snakes, or unicorns.

And then again, at your very feet, in the damp blackness of the turf among the roots of the sycamore, who knows what is going on down there? Worms may be confessing, beetles may be at war, or there may be strange slugs or caterpillars unknown to science. Who knows? And all these surmises and astonishments, these glimpses of the arcane, emerge from the shade of that grand old sycamore, which doesn't give a damn anyway, and stands there serene, majestic and, I hope, amused by the kaleidoscope of life itself, in truth or in dream . . .

But my mind wanders. What was I saying? I must be getting old.

I almost decided yesterday, as I concluded Day 126 of this performance, to bring the curtain down, write 'Finis' or call 'Time, Gentlemen, please!' I rather liked the idea that the poet Marvell suggested for his racier divinities – of concluding life's career motionless in a tree, e.g. in yesterday's sycamore! But no, as he also reminds me, it's a wondrous life is this I lead, so here we go again.

It's a lovely morning once more, and my theme today is one of gratitude. I walk with a stick nowadays, my balance being wobbly, and it is heart-warming how this declaration of infirmity is greeted by one and all – not just by my dear Welsh fellow citizens, but by unlikely strangers wherever I go. Gigantic lorries stop to let me cross the street! Wild, uncouth youths keep doors open for me! Men with nasty faces help me up steps, and evident harridans offer me gaps in queues.

I can offer these benefactors nothing in return. We shall never see each other again. Just the stick does it, and they are simply honouring the instincts of their own hearts and confirming my own conviction that the human race everywhere essentially prefers to be decent.

One of the very best men I have ever known is a nonconformist minister almost exactly the same age as I am – which means, in my own agnostic view, that it's probably nearly time to pack our bags for a final exit. He would certainly not agree, being a profoundly dedicated Christian still famously active in his cause.

Like everyone else, I greatly admire him and his dear wife. Their lives have been rich, rewarding and distinguished, but not without sorrows, and as a hot sceptic I think they are lovely examples of an opposite persuasion, gently practising what they preach.

Nevertheless, I was not surprised to learn last week that this good man had collapsed and been taken to hospital. Holy he undoubtedly is, but in my view the grim reaper recognizes no faiths and no merits, and the news came as no shock to me. Twice I called his dear partner for news of his condition, and twice the prognosis was as I expected – even the truest and most faithful of Christians is not immune to Nature. I rang twice more, and each time the end seemed closer, but when I rang for the fifth time, the response was different. Not only was the answering voice almost chirpily nonchalant, it was also unmistakably the voice of my dear old friend himself, not dying at all, not despairing in the least, but home from the hospital, faithful as always to his beliefs, and no doubt confident anyway, as his doctrine assures him, of another life to come.

Of course he is going to go in the end, like you and me and everyone else, but just for a moment or two, when I heard his cheerful voice that afternoon – just for a moment I wavered in my scepticism . . .

DAY 129

I cannot deny that I find it harder every year to get up in the morning, but I have learnt to cheer the ordeal by making it an old-school, all-American occasion.

This I achieve through the medium of the first American I ever met. Eighty-odd years ago, towards the end of the Second World War, I was waiting to join the British Army by working as a temporary cub reporter on a newspaper in Bristol. One day there arrived at that war-ravaged seaport, in a convoy from New York, an American Army road show, on a morale-building tour. I was detailed by the *Western Daily Press* to interview the show's producer, and so I became briefly acquainted with Irving Berlin.

He was delightfully kind to his callow interviewer, my very, very first American, and he remains to this day my ideal archetypal citizen of the great republic. He had worked his way from being a singing waiter in a New York Chinese restaurant to being both the composer and the lyricist of songs that are loved and sung around the world to this day – literally hundreds of them in the collected volume of his works that I have in my library now.

And among those Irving Berlin songs is my morning reveille, from the show he brought to Bristol that day, which cheerfully assures its soldier audience that one day the wretched bugler who wakes them up each morning, like the guy who wakes *him* up, is going to be murdered on their behalf.

Of course I don't feel murderous. On the contrary. Already that merrily sardonic lyric, with its irresistible tune, has got me out of bed singing and feeling musically young, and in a particularly American way – Irving Berlin's way, an old American way, that is, from the glory days of the Great Republic, when it still felt young too, and proud of itself, singing among friends in the morning.

DAY 130

Aspects of an Addiction

The fascination of Wales is a phenomenon widely recognized but frequently baffling. Everyone knows how proud to be Welsh Welsh people can be, but even the Welshest of them can be hard put to analyse the nature of their pride. What is it about Wales, then? The landscape perhaps? The history? The language? But many of the Welsh live in ordinary or even unlovely surroundings, and most of them speak little Welsh.

So? What is the compelling nature of Welshness, in the abstract? Why is it so vivid? Why did Shakespeare, writing about his archetypal Welshman, feel the need to assure us that there was true potency behind the bluster of Fluellen? Welsh people often put it all down to the abstraction called *hiraeth*, which dictionaries translate simply as longing, or nostalgia. I myself think of it, though, as a sort of national addiction, more subtle, more complex, and being half Welsh, half English myself, in my hybrid way I often contemplate its jumbled fascinations . . .

Geography, of course, is part of it. In a way, Wales is an island, but characteristically an island that is not an island. It is bounded on only three sides by the sea, and its neo-islanders are not often insular. Welsh patriotism, though frequently ardent, is seldom racist, except for occasional simmerings of Anglophobia, often brought on by the insidious infiltration of tourism. Foreigners have generally been welcomed here, and often admired. Black Jack was the rage of the girls in eighteenth-century Cricieth, in the north; the black community of Cardiff's Tiger Bay flourishes to this day in the south; and many enterprising Jews have succeeded in this essentially Christian society. Of course, there must be bigots here – where aren't there? Even Tiger Bay had its race riots a hundred years ago, but bigotry is not, one may say, very Welsh!

Perhaps the truth is that Welshness is essentially an idea, or rather a confusion or concert of ideas, blended down all the generations, powerful enough to create images, influence emotions, dictate behaviours and create symbols from century to century. Welshness is the power of language and landscape, the fascination of legend, the unfailing allures of comradeship, community and possession. Welshness is Saints and Footballers, Poets and Wizards and Goats and Miners and Singers and Fairies and magical confusions – all are always with us addicts in Wales, the Land of our Fathers, and the grand old country itself is not only as tough as it is beautiful, but full of humour, too.

So, after all, who would *not* be hooked?

Also by Jan Morris

In My Mind's Eye

I have never before in my life kept a diary of my thoughts, and here at the start of my ninth decade, having for the moment nothing much else to write, I am having a go at it. Good luck to me . . .

So begins this extraordinary book, the first collection of diary pieces from one of the great chroniclers of the last sixty years. Jan Morris shares her day-to-day thoughts on the world over the course of one year. From cats to cars, travel to home, classical music to the great American songbook, Wales to the British Empire, marmalade to Meghan Markle, the decline of the 'special relationship' to the spectre of Brexit, and of course books, her own and others', this is a cornucopia of delights from a unique and treasured literary figure.

'A wonderfully wise collection . . . After closing the book I felt bereft of Morris's company.' *Sunday Herald*

'A thing of wonder: a diary of daily musings with zero pretension. It is light yet profound, ecstatic yet melancholy, ethereal yet droll.' *Evening Standard*

'A splendidly quirky confection that mixes the trivial with the serious, like life.' *Literary Review*

faber

Also by Jan Morris

A Writer's World: Travels 1950–2000

In a wonderfully evocative collection of her travel writing and reportage from over five decades, Jan Morris has produced a unique portrait of the late twentieth century – from New York to Venice, from the first ascent of Everest to the fall of the Berlin Wall.

'A reminder of just how entertaining, how informative and how thought-provoking a restless, inquisitive, experienced writer can be.' *Sunday Times*

'Wherever Morris goes, she brings a sharp, impassioned yet subtle eye, and an inexhaustible love of adventure . . . There are few better ways to see the world than in her company.' *Daily Telegraph*

'Time and again, Morris finds delicious ways of conveying the personality of a place . . . This is a five-star portrait of our planet.' *Daily Express*

faber

Also by Jan Morris

Conundrum

As one of Britain's best and most-loved travel writers, Jan Morris has led an extraordinary life. Perhaps her most remarkable work is this grippingly honest account of her ten-year transition from man to woman – its pains and joys, its frustrations and discoveries. On first publication in 1974, the book generated enormous interest around the world and was chosen by *The Times* as one of the '100 Key Books of Our Time'.

'Fascinating in its shrewdness, warmth and honesty . . . Fresh and alive and beautifully told.' *Observer*

'The best first-hand account ever written by a traveller across the boundaries of sex.' *Daily Mail*

'*Conundrum* is above all the record of a journey, with self-knowledge as its destination . . . A collected, mystical and often very funny book.' *The Times*

faber

Also by Jan Morris

Trieste and the Meaning of Nowhere

In *Trieste and the Meaning of Nowhere*, Jan Morris has crafted a sublime meditation on a most unusual city. Jan Morris (then James) first visited Trieste as a soldier at the end of the Second World War. Since then, the city has come to represent her own life, with all its hopes, disillusionments, loves and memories.

'A poignant and enchanting evocation of a life, inspired by a beautifully written meditation on a unique city. A gem.' P. D. James

'Exquisite . . . Most travel books tell you about a journey that gets you to a place. *Trieste and the Meaning of Nowhere* tells you about a place that leads you to a journey.' *Evening Standard*

'An exquisitely well-crafted book . . . Morris has erudition and a waywardly original sensibility, and she writes not just sentences, not just paragraphs, but whole chapters consummately graceful both in sound and sense.' *Sunday Times*

faber

Also by Jan Morris

Venice

An impassioned portrait of one of the world's most glorious cities by 'one of the greatest living writers' (*The Times*). Divided into three sections which explore the Venetian people, the city itself and the lagoon on which it stands, *Venice* enriches any visit to that great city – be it in person, or simply in the mind. Since its first publication, *Venice* has appeared in many editions and has become an international bestseller.

'The best book about Venice ever written.' *Sunday Times*

'No sensible visitor should visit the place without it . . . *Venice* stands alone as the essential introduction, and as a work of literature in its own right.' *Observer*

'For those to whom Venice is a memory, a treat in store, or even a dream, the broad canvas of this book, covering a thousand years in the life of the one of the most complex, original and active communities the world has ever seen, is a work of lasting interest.' *Guardian*

faber